DATE DUE

THE STORY of the
LITTLE BIG HORN

A Civil War portrait of Brevet Major-General George Armstrong Custer, lieutenant-colonel of the Seventh Cavalry, killed in action at the Little Big Horn, June 25, 1876. This is probably Custer's best portrait. During the 1876 campaign, however, his yellow hair was cut short, and he dressed in buckskin.

THE STORY of the LITTLE BIG HORN

Custer's Last Fight

BY

Colonel W. A. Graham

JUDGE ADVOCATE, U. S. ARMY, RETIRED

University of Nebraska Press
Lincoln and London

First Bison Book printing: 1988
Most recent printing indicated by the first digit below:
1   2   3   4   5   6   7   8   9   10

Library of Congress Cataloging-in-Publication Data
Graham, W. A. (William Alexander), 1875–1954.
   The story of the Little Big Horn: Custer's last fight /
by W.A. Graham.
   p.   cm.
   Reprint. Originally published: New York: Century
Co., 1926.
ISBN 0-8032-2132-0.   ISBN 0-8032-7026-7 (pbk.)
   1. Little Big Horn, Battle of the, 1876.   2. Custer,
George Armstrong, 1839–1876. I. Title.
E83.876.G73 1988   CIP 87–30129
973.8´2—dc19

Reprinted by arrangement with Stackpole Books

PREFACE TO SECOND EDITION

Since 1926, when this narrative of the Seventh Cavalry's defeat at the hands of the followers of Sitting Bull was first offered to the public, much has been written on the subject, by numerous authors of varying ability.

The story of Custer's Last Fight—the story of the Little Big Horn—and the mystery that still enshrouds Custer's fate, continue to fascinate the student of our Indian Wars. It is a subject that strangely evokes the interest of each succeeding generation, despite the fact that two-thirds of a century has now elapsed since the Yellow Hair and his cohorts passed into history.

Little that is new, and nothing of any moment has been discovered since 1926; and as the years pass, it becomes increasingly unlikely that anything of importance will be discovered. For that reason, and because nearly all those who participated in the fight, officers, soldiers and Indians alike, have now crossed the great divide, the author has found necessary only minor changes in the text, changes that affect the narrative and the substance not at all. Both remain precisely as originally written.

The book has received both praise and criticism, as was to be expected. On the whole, however, it has stood the test of the years, and is again offered as the author's earnest and unbiased effort to present an accurate word-picture of the greatest of all combats between the American Soldier and the American Indian.

The notes refer to the date of original publication, 1926; except Note 9½, which has been added.

FOREWORD TO SECOND EDITION

The Battle of the Little Big Horn was a dramatic and romantic tragedy. It has provoked more speculation and more controversy than any other military episode in our history. It has a fascination for the military student that is unique. The wild and lonely country, the distance at that time from all settlements and all aid, the savage and fierce character of the Indian foe and his overwhelming numbers, as well as the great mystery which has forever shrouded the movements and actions of Custer's little command, and the manner in which he and five troops of the 7th Cavalry met their deaths with not a single survivor, have excited the imagination and interest of soldiers and civilians alike for over sixty years.

Custer was a popular military hero in this country. His defeat and the annihilation of his command shocked his associates and admirers. Newspaper and magazine writers, especially in the West, wrote the wildest and most improbable stories. They looked for a scapegoat and selected Major Reno toward whom great injustice was done. Much controversy ensued between those who supported Custer's actions, so far as they were known, and those who criticized him.

For years afterwards many civilian writers, claiming to have interviewed Indians who took part in the battle, wrote fantastic stories. Claims were made that survivors —soldiers or Indian scouts—had been found. The people of the country were given utterly wrong descriptions of the whole campaign.

Not until Col. W. A. Graham's book appeared was there a true, logical, sane and dispassionate account given to the Army and the public. Col. Graham states the facts as known. His conjectures are given as conjectures. The evidence is given and the reader can decide debatable questions for himself.

This book is a valuable military document and an instructive and intensely interesting tale that every soldier should have in his library and that neither soldier nor civilian can put down, once he has started the reading of it.

H H Hawkins

Brigadier-General, United States Army, Retired.

Washington, D. C.,
May 15, 1941.

THE FAMOUS "ANHEUSER-BUSCH" PAINTING OF "CUSTER'S LAST STAND," FAMILIAR TO ALL OLD TIME WESTERN HOTELS AND BAR ROOMS

The Original picture was destroyed by fire June 13, 1946.

This original canvas was painted by Cassily Adams, and was nine feet, six inches wide and sixteen feet, five inches long. The painting was painted on a canvas wagon cover issued by the Ordnance company at that time. It was hung in the Post Officers' Club at Fort Bliss, Texas, for the reason that the 7th Cavalry had no building large enough to display it. Mr. Adams painted the picture according to Scout Curley's version of the battle of the Little Big Horn, June 25, 1876.

The 7th Cavalry regimental history files show that Mr. Adams completed the painting in 1888, and sold it to a John Ferber who owned a saloon in St. Louis, Mo., in which the painting hung for approximately six years. The late Adolphus Busch, Sr., desired a scene that depicted the west and purchased the painting from the estate of the late Mr. Ferber in 1892, and displayed it in the Anheuser Busch, Inc., reception room. According to Mr. Busch the painting was purchased at the price of $35,000.

At the outbreak of the Spanish American War in 1898, Mr. Busch presented the painting to the Seventh Cavalry, then stationed at Fort Riley, Kansas. The presentation took place during the ceremony in the old consolidated Mess Hall (now the Post Exchange Building), at Fort Riley. Captain J. M. Bell, Regimental Adjutant, 7th Cavalry, acted as Chairman and Colonel George A. Forsythe, Regimental Commander at that time, received the picture in behalf of the regiment. A number of officers who participated in the battle of the Little Big Horn were present at the ceremony and made speeches describing the battle.

During the period from 1909 to 1922 the picture was rolled on a tent pole and stored in the Quartermaster Warehouse at Fort Bliss, Texas, as the regiment was constantly changing station during this period. In 1922 the painting was retrieved from the Quartermaster warehouse by the 7th Cavalry Regimental Supply Officer and placed in the Regimental Supply storeroom until 1934; at this time it was unrolled and arrangements were made for the renovation of the painting.

This picture was renovated by Mr. Raymond O. Richards, Assistant Director, Federal Art Project, November 14, 1938, at Fort Bliss, Texas.

INTRODUCTION

In the summer of 1866 the Congress of the United States, after much discussion, reorganized and enlarged the fighting force of the regular army, the cavalry and infantry being increased respectively to ten regiments where there had been but six, and forty-five battalions where numerically there had been but nineteen.

Though the entire array was not to exceed 45,000 men, this startling extravagance was speedily assailed by pacifists, economists, etc., as utterly unnecessary, "now that the war was over"; and it followed that within three remorseful years the builders of what was to have become the bulwark of our national defense were as busy tearing down as they had been precipitate in bracing up, and in the summer of 1869 officers by scores went back to civil life as the infantry was telescoped into twenty-five old-style regiments, a year's pay being bestowed on each man thus eliminated: and as this process did not of itself bring about the desired reduction, certain devious and dubious methods were prescribed, whereby officers with shady pasts (and quite a few without) found themselves suddenly and summarily out of the army, turned loose upon a cold and unsympathetic world.

As it had been prescribed that all vacancies thus created in the cavalry and artillery should be filled from what had been named "the unassigned list," promotion became blocked for more than a generation.

And still the reduction fell short of the demands of Congress, even, as was said in a certain summer, "with such aid as was afforded by our all-too-eager red brothers," the warriors of our Western domain. Far to the south on the Texan border-land Kiowa and Comanche afforded many a casualty. In Arizona the elusive Apache clipped off many a promising life. All along the cross-bordered Smoky Hill route to Denver, the Cheyennes, fiercest of the wild frontier cavalry, harassed the big wagon trains headed and heralded as for "Pike's Peak or Bust"; and still farther north, along the Platte to Independence Rock and beyond—the old Mormon trail to the new Salt Lake city—several thousand strong, the warlike Sioux, under their warrior chief Red Cloud, played havoc with unguarded outfits.

It was this condition of affairs that induced the Congress to maintain in such undue proportion the cavalry branch of the army. It was a fact that while many a blanket in the artillery and infantry remained tenantless, the cavalry rode with full ranks. There was a time when it was asserted that at the heels of certain favored and favorite regiments, there followed, by the dozen, eager and adventurous spirits, young men of American parentage, ready and eager to sign enlistment papers the moment a vacancy occurred. It is another fact that while four fifths of our horsemen were stationed all over the wild West and Texas, one fifth, just two regiments, were retained in close touch with civilization—the Fifth—the old Second Cavalry of antebellum days, and the Seventh, newly organized, yet already leaping into martial prominence.

Quartered in and about the city of Washington and the slowly reviving municipalities of the Southeast, the Fifth Cavalry was scattered by troop over the most attractive sections of the country, while the Seventh occupied stations like Forts Leavenworth and Riley in Kansas, under the inspiration, guidance, and leadership of their lieutenant-colonel—the most conspicuous soldier of the time in the army of the United States.

INTRODUCTION

George Armstrong Custer, foot of his class at West Point and so regardless of academic regulations that it became a mooted question in the spring of 1861 whether or not he should be awarded the prized diploma. So, while his classmates were hurried away to Washington and set at once to work drilling the rapidly assembling regiments of militia, Custer was held back. But "Custer's luck," a commodity in which he ever expressed supreme confidence, soon directed his wayward footsteps. He "followed on" in time to get into the thick of the scrimmage at First Bull Run, and thereafter by leaps and bounds, to rise from one command to another, to the end that by July, 1863, he rode at the head of the new Michigan brigade of cavalry, and in the spring of '65 was a division commander.

It was in the nine days from Five Forks to Appomattox that Custer was in his glory. Leader of the Third Division of the Cavalry

Corps of the Army of the Potomac, which swore by him, clad in a picturesque garb of his own devising, bestriding a big mettlesome charger as full of energy and vim as was its rider, he hovered every mile along the southward flank of the retiring remnants of Lee's heroic army, darting in at every cross-road, picking off flankers, stragglers, wagons by the dozen, even occasional field-guns and caissons, giving the starving columns no chance to eat, much less to sleep, striking everywhere along the line of march, interposing wherever he found a gap, compelling his adversary to halt and deploy, thereby delaying the progress of the gray columns and enabling the infantry of the Army of the Potomac to come striding along by every parallel road, gradually overhauling their gallant but exhausted foemen, capturing whole batteries of field-artillery, and finally, in one supreme effort, throwing his entire division athwart the Confederate front, and compelling a dead halt until the Union infantry could reach the extreme head of the column, reach around and across the turnpikes and roads, and finally, screened by Custer's cavalry, halt their long dusty columns and form their lines of battle facing eastward —square across the Confederates' only way to safety.

Thus and then at last the almost indomitable army of the South was brought to bay, and Lee's dramatic surrender followed. It was Custer who had the luck to be in the lead at the start and to hold it against all comers to the finish; Custer who led the last charge of Sheridan's cavalry (against that South Carolina colonel who wouldn't surrender) ; Custer who bore away in triumph the table on which Grant had drawn up the terms of that merciful disbandment of Lee's devoted men; Custer, whose runaway charger made him by long odds the most conspicuous object at the grand review in Washington; Custer whose yellow curls and major-general's uniform in the fourth carriage of the presidential procession, one year later, drew the enthusiastic plaudits of the crowds along their route—crowds that had not so much as a single hand or cheer for Andrew Johnson, chief magistrate of the victorious Union; and finally Custer who became the magnet that lured to his standard hundreds of daring young Americans; for when the Seventh Cavalry took the field against the hostiles of the southern plains, Custer at the head of the column, it was practically an American regiment, one in which the soldier of foreign birth was almost a stranger. The roster of the Seventh Cavalry was made up in greater number—probably far greater —than any other in the army of the United States, of eager young troopers, American to the core.

Yet all had not gone well or happily with

the fortunes of the Seventh. The battle of the Washita against Black Kettle's overwhelming array of warriors, starting vaingloriously with the band blaring Custer's battle-song of Garry Owen—gallant Lou Hamilton falling in the initial charge—and to the dumb amaze of some of his best officers, closing with the abandonment to their cruel fate of Major Elliott and his flanking party as Custer withdrew the regiment, never again to hold its undivided faith or admiration. Then came the episode of his courtmartial in Kansas for deliberate absence and the summary shooting down of deserters in the field, and later the splitting up into scattered troops during the Ku-Klux days and the troublous political times in the South.

Matters seemed brighter, however, when the reunited Seventh made its long northward march to Fort Abraham Lincoln. Yet again in the spring of '76, its restless leader brought

down upon himself the censure of the War
Department and the peremptory orders of the
President removing him from command at the
very opening of the greatest campaign against
the hostile Sioux ever yet undertaken, and his
reinstatement only upon his earnest pleading,
and the request of the department commander, General Terry, that Custer might be
spared the infinite humiliation of retention at
the rear when his gallant regiment took the
field, ōn the campaign that every officer believed destined to decide whether the red man
or the paleface should thereafter be master of
the Western world.

With unknown numbers assembled at his
call, Sitting Bull had defied every overture of
the Indian Bureau, and at least six tribes of
the great Sioux nation had joined him on the
war-path. Ogalallas, Brulés, Minneconjous,
and Hunkpapás from the southern limits of
their broad domain; Sans Arcs and Blackfeet

from the northward; and with them, most to
be dreaded, those skilled allies, the Northern
Cheyennes. Scouts and frontiersmen had located them vaguely as somewhere in the glorious hill country between the Big Horn Mountains and the Yellowstone, and what was most
significant and as it proved most fatal, in the
ten years that had elapsed since Red Cloud
with his thousands, though scantily armed,
had lured and massacred to the last man the
little battalion sent forth from "the hated fort
on the Piney," the Sioux had learned the use
of modern weapons. Only muzzle-loaders
had either white or red warrior in that bitter
December of 1866; but in the famous "wagon-
box battle," some months thereafter, Captain
Powell, with the first issue of Springfield
breech-loaders, had given the Sioux their first
lesson in the possibilities of warfare with the
paleface. Then came the decade in which all
over the wide Indian frontier, with the full

knowledge if not connivance of the servants of one department of our paternal government, the red wards of the nation were gradually supplied with the latest model repeating-arms and ammunition, wherewith to combat and at times to overcome the sworn soldiery of another. In plain words, through the Indian agencies, north, south, and west, "for hunting purposes" of course, the red warriors of the most famous tribes became possessors not only of the single-shooting rifle or carbine, as issued to our infantry and cavalry, but, far more effective, the Henry or Winchester magazine-rifle, wherewith, anywhere within six hundred yards, to pump leaden missiles into the ranks of our devoted troopers— a vast advantage over their luckless foe.

Summer after summer, loading up with these modern arms of the best make, enterprising fellow-citizens steamed away up the Missouri, meeting their Indian customers at well known rendezvous, and there bartering their weapons at standard rates—one hundred dollars' worth of robes, hides, or furs—buffalo, bear, or beaver—the price demanded for either Henry or Winchester; and according to distance, ten, fifteen, or twenty cents' worth, as the price of a single cartridge; then back to St. Louis, the old home of the Astor Fur Company, to dispose of their valuable cargoes.

So too, at the agencies, every brave sought to be the owner of a magazine-rifle; and "for hunting purposes" why should they be denied? In that decade too, chiefs without number sought opportunity to visit the national capital, to pay their respects to the Great White Father, and return laden with death-dealing gifts by no means unsolicited. It was recorded of one of the number that on the occasion of his visit to the White House and his truculent demand to be furnished with the latest model of the Winchester—not only

for himself, but for each warrior of his impos-
ing retinue—when some prominent function-
ary expressed the hope that the desired weapons were not for the purpose of "killing my
soldiers," he made prompt and disdainful response that "a club was all he needed for
that."

Deny these statements as some at least of
the officials of the Indian Bureau occasionally
did, the fact remains that between the date
of the Wagon Box battle early in '67, and the
triumphant summer of '76, nine out of ten of
the warriors known to be on the war-path had
not only the magazine-rifle, with abundant
supply of copper cartridges, but, as a rule,
two revolvers, Colt's Navy preferred. The
very few dead that fell into the hands of our
troopers fairly bristled with deadly weapons.

As for ammunition, even as late as mid-
June in the battle summer of '76, it was being
freighted by wagon-load to the agencies far

inland; and just as the red man was supplied with superior weapons for frontier warfare, so had he a more reliable cartridge than had been issued to some, at least, of our cavalry; some to the Seventh certainly, for during the following year there were Indians, employed as scouts, who told our fellows in the field of numbers of Custer's devoted followers, on that fatal twenty-fifth of June, seen vainly hacking with their hunting-knives at cartridge-shells wedged in the heated carbine chambers —shells through whose rim the extractor of the Springfield carbine had cut its way as though through so much putty.

It had not opened well, that centennial summer, which saw by tens of thousands our citizens flocking to Philadelphia for the first of our great expositions. Early in March, even on Patrick's day, in face of a raging blizzard, with the mercury at thirty degrees below, a strong column of cavalry rode northward

from old Fort Fetterman on the Platte, in
hope of striking in their winter lodges a band
of Sioux under the lead of one of the bravest
and brainiest of their war chiefs—Ta Shunka
Witko—Crazy Horse—against whom had
been pitted a war-time major-general, one of
Grant's own classmates. And within the
week that double-starred yet ill-starred soldier, brave, loyal, dutiful, yet utterly inexpe-
rienced, meeting with unlooked-for disaster,
drifted back to the Platte with a crop of courts
martial as the sole fruits of the enterprise.

Then, roused to strenuous efforts, the War
Department, determining to deal a blow that
the disdainful chiefs would rue to their dying
day, had directed almost every available soldier from the northern stations to concentrate
on that red army toward which were turned
the eyes of the eager young braves of every
tribe between the Missouri and the Platte on
the south and the Big Horn on the west.

INTRODUCTION

From Fort Lincoln came General Terry with a strong column of infantry, and a battery of Gatling guns; and with him, Custer and every troop of the war-tried Seventh, by that time, after many seasons in the field, the most experienced regiment in mounted warfare of the entire army. Westward they came by long day marches from opposite Bismarck—on to the Yellowstone—the Powder—the Tongue —the Rosebud. Eastward from the Montana stations came another veteran commander of the Civil War, John Gibbon, with the Seventh Infantry and squadrons of the Second Horse. Finally, marching northward from the posts along the Union Pacific and the North Platte, most formidable of all in point of numbers, came the Third Cavalry, with a supporting squadron of the Second, and a composite regiment made up from the Fourth, Ninth, and Fourteenth Regiments, under the lead of the only man who had prevailed over the Apache, who had spent the best years of his life among the Indians of the Pacific slope, and of whom, perhaps, the most was expected —George Crook—to whom the Sioux and the Cheyenne as yet were strangers.

It was Crook who was destined to strike the first blow of the new campaign, Crook who was first to lead a heavy force against the most warlike Indians in the world. Even as Sheridan had planned, Crook confidently marched on to the heart of "Indian story land," drove in confidently to the attack, and in one hour learned a lesson that revolution-ized his idea of the prowess of the Sioux. At the end of that hour he was glad to be able to extricate his command, to fall back to his intrenched camp, there to double his defensive measures and send back to the States for re-inforcements.

And thus there came a comrade regiment from beyond Crook's department limits—thus came Sheridan himself, far out to Fort Laramie, personally to send them in, with orders to stop the flow of warriors, arms, ammunition, and supplies from the Red Cloud Agency to Sitting Bull's triumphant camps. Thus it happened that there came to the Fifth Cavalry, on the very day of his promotion to its head, Wesley Merritt, Custer's senior and rival division commander at Five Forks and Appomattox. And thus, having broken up the travois traffic to the west of the Black Hills of Dakota, waiting for orders at Sage Creek, Merritt and the Fifth, on the early morning of the seventh of July, 1876, were stunned by the awful tidings brought by Lieutenant Hall and Buffalo Bill—"Custer and five whole troops wiped off the face of the earth!"

For half a century, both in and out of the army, vain search has been made for some one volume in which should appear the story of that deplorable event. We have heard or read individual experiences by the dozens, but never until now has there appeared a complete, comprehensive, and reliable account of that fatal campaign. It is the work of an officer accustomed for years to weigh evidence, and he has taken that of almost every survivor who could be reached; and having sifted and winnowed the tangled mass, partially from the records of the Reno Court of Inquiry, in 1879, but largely from the volume of replies from letters to and interviews with participants in the campaign, with the facile pen of the ready writer whose heart is in his work, whose objective has been the truth, the whole truth, and nothing but the truth, there is laid before the reading public a book of absorbing interest from cover to cover, utterly free from favor or prejudice, a narrative as clear to the layman as to the professional, closing with an array of notes and authorities that challenge criticism or question, and accompanied by

sketch-maps, which enable the reader to follow every move of that devoted band, faithful to their soldier oath of service, the one
complete and reliable record yet to appear of
Custer's Last Battle.

Charles King

Brig. Gen. U. S. Vols.

General King, the most famous writer of stories of life in the "Old Army",
deceased in 1933.

FOREWORD

Colonel Graham has spent several years in the study of the battle of the Little Big Horn, and has interviewed nearly all of the known survivors of that disaster.

In my opinion the following account is as nearly accurate as it is possible to make it at this late day, and contains all the facts of importance that will ever be known.

In saying, "The chief cause of disaster was unquestionably the lack of correct information as to the numbers, the organization, and the equipment of the Indians," he hit the nail squarely on the head; for if these things had been known, General Terry would not have divided his command at the mouth of the Rosebud, nor would General Custer have made two divisions of his regiment, one fif-

teen miles from the village and the other when
the village was about two miles away.

The idea that the Indians would try to escape was general in the Seventh Cavalry on
the morning of June 25, and the first division
was made in order to catch them in whatever
direction they might run.

General Custer undoubtedly believed they
were running away when he decided to move
down the right flank of the river and attack
on the flank instead of following in Reno's
rear.

The remark of Girard, the interpreter, to
Custer, "There are your Indians, running like
the devil," of Sergeant Knipe, "We've got
'em, boys," as he rode past Benteen's squadron,
and the trumpeter Martin's, "the Indians were
surprised and are skedaddling," show what the
general impression was in Custer's command
at the time he moved off down the right bank.

Even if the blame for the disaster was due

FOREWORD

to General Custer, the fact remains that he
and his five troops died heroic and glorious
deaths, and upheld the reputation of their
regiment and the United States Army, for
bravery in action.

Brigadier-General, United States Army,
Retired.
Cooperstown, New York,
September 2, 1925.

General Edgerly, deceased in 1927.

ILLUSTRATIONS

ILLUSTRATIONS

ILLUSTRATIONS

THE STORY OF THE LITTLE
BIG HORN

THE STORY OF THE LITTLE BIG HORN

I

THE men of the Golden West have ever been a forward-looking people; else the past fifty years, which has seen it develop from a land inhabited by savages, to become the pride, the wonder, and the backbone of America, could not have produced, in so short a time, those results that have amazed the world. Forward; always forward; overcoming, trampling down, sweeping aside all obstacles, the men of the West have marched on. Such is the spirit of the West.

The history of those fifty years is replete with the records of glorious achievement, the fruits of which the younger generation accepts and enjoys, little knowing, and perhaps, little caring, how its heritage was won. This is the tale of but one of the many events which blaze the trail; one which the Western youth may well pause to look back upon, since it marked the high tide of the red man's struggle against the onward rush of civilization, and stands out, in all the history of America, as the greatest victory ever won by the Indian warrior over the white soldier; a greater triumph, even, than was Braddock's Defeat.

In 1868, the Government concluded a treaty with the Dakotas (the Indians generally known and referred to as the Sioux Nation), which set off to that numerous and warlike people a large territory in the Northwest to be their own forever. It included their favorite hunting-grounds, the Black Hills, and certain lands adjoining; and the Sioux, for the most part, were satisfied.

Tatanka-I-Yotanka, "Sitting Bull," the Hunkpapa
medicine man, political leader of the non-treaty
Sioux in 1876.

Then came the discovery of gold in the Black Hills, and the inevitable resulting inroads of covetous whites.

In 1874, an expedition under the command of Major-General George A. Custer was sent into the Black Hills by the Government, to reconnoiter and explore the country. The Sioux, quite naturally, became perturbed and resentful over this invasion of their lands; and during the year 1875, their protests having gone unheeded, it became apparent that resistance was imminent. Some few of the Dakotas had never accepted the treaty of 1868, and to these malcontents were now joined hundreds of protestants against the violation of their treaty rights.

Foremost among the "non-treaty" Sioux, the leader and rallying-point of all the dissatisfied and rebellious, was the Hunkpapá medicine-man, Sitting Bull; and to him, somewhere in the Rosebud country in Montana, during the early part of 1876, flocked thousands of representatives from the many tribes of the Sioux Nation: Hunkpapá; Brulé; Ogalalla; Minneconjou; Sans Arc; Yanktonnais; Santee; Blackfeet—all were there. The Cheyenne and Arapahoe, allied nations, sent active aid in numerous array. How many were with him, no one knew; nor, for reasons of their own, did the Indian agents wish to have it known.

In November, 1875, the hostile attitude of Sitting Bull and his followers moved the commissioner of Indian affairs to recommend that force be used to compel these bands to "cease marauding and settle down, as the other Sioux have done," and the Indian Inspector called for the use of troops, "this winter, the sooner the better." In December, 1875, the Interior Department notified the hostiles that if they failed to come in by January 31, 1876, the military would be sent against them: and on

February 1, the appointed time having arrived without response, the whole situation was turned over to be dealt with by the War Department. General Sheridan, then commanding the Division of the Missouri with headquarters at Chicago, was instructed to reduce the hostiles to subjection.

During February and March, 1876, a part of General Crook's column under Colonel J. J. Reynolds was sent into the Powder River country and encountered the Indians under Crazy Horse, but this expedition was without satisfactory result; and Sheridan thereupon organized a campaign from three directions: south, west, and east, to be under the command of Generals Crook, Gibbon, and Custer.

Major-General George A. Custer, to whom command of the eastern column had been entrusted, was one of the most brilliant military figures of his time. Graduating from the Military Academy at West Point with the

[7]

class of June, 1861, he began his career as an officer of the army at the disastrous battle of Bull Run: but by sheer merit and the force of an extraordinary personality he had steadily risen in his chosen profession until he became one of the recognized leaders among the cavalry commanders of the Civil War. His elevation to high rank had been unprecedented; and when made a major-general of volunteers in command of a division of cavalry, he was the youngest man who had ever held that rank in the American Army since the Revolutionary War, when the youthful Marquis de Lafayette, representative of the King of France, received similar recognition at the hands of the Continental Congress.

Before the eastern column got under way, however, Custer gave offense to General Grant, then President of the United States, by becoming involved in the impeachment proceedings pending against Secretary of

War Belknap, who had resigned under fire. By the President's order Custer was summarily removed from command; and General Alfred H. Terry, the Department commander, was ordered by Sheridan to go in his stead. To his great humiliation, Custer was forbidden to accompany the expedition in any capacity whatever.

The Seventh Cavalry, which formed the important part of the eastern column, was a comparatively new regiment, having been organized after the close of the Civil War. Its commanding officer, Sturgis, was at this time on detached service, as were also the two senior majors of the regiment. General Custer, normally second in command, was thus the senior officer on duty with the organization; and next under him was Marcus A. Reno, the junior major.

Among the troop commanders were men who had made brilliant records as leaders of cavalry during the Civil War, and several who had held command of regiments and even of brigades. There existed, unfortuntely, much jealousy in the regiment, which had become a house divided against itself, separated into Custer and anti-Custer factions. Chief among the latter was Colonel Frederick W. Benteen, commander of H Troop; and second only to him was Major Reno.

Upon being removed from command of the expedition, Custer had made frantic efforts for reinstatement; and through the kindly intercession of General Terry, the President at the last moment lifted the ban. Custer was allowed to go at the head of his regiment, but Terry remained in command of the expedition.

That Custer chafed under such restraint cannot be doubted, nor is it much to be wondered at. His was a bold, free, impulsive character, in whom dash and audacity were as second nature, and to whom subordination to another's will was onerous. His rise to military eminence had been both rapid and extraordinary; his commands had been large and important; his independence rarely fettered. He doubtless felt that the President's action had been as arbitrary as it was humiliating: he took the field smarting under a sense of injustice; and that his state of mind in some degree affected the manner in which he conducted his campaign, cannot be doubted.

The eastern column, under the command of General Terry, marched from Fort Abraham Lincoln, near Bismarck, North Dakota, May 17, 1876, and reached a point some twenty-five miles above the mouth of the Powder River, on the Yellowstone, June 10. From this point Terry despatched Major Reno, with six troops of the Seventh, to scout the valleys of the Powder and Tongue rivers in search of the hostiles. Though not contemplated by his orders, Reno swung west as far as the Rosebud, and there discovered a fresh trail leading up that stream.   This he followed for a short distance, and then, retracing his steps, cut across the country to the command near the mouth of the Rosebud, its point of confluence with the Yellowstone.   Here General Terry, on June 21, after receiving Reno's report, held a conference on board the supply-steamer *Far West*, and laid out the plan of his intended operations to Gibbon and Custer, his two subordinates.   (Note 1.)

In brief, the plan was that Gibbon, whose column of about four hundred men was composed largely of infantry, should proceed south along the banks of the Big Horn River, some fifty miles to the west, while Custer, with the entire Seventh Cavalry, would ride south, up the Rosebud, until he reached the trail which Reno had discovered on the scouting trip a few days before.   He was then to

"Mitch" Bouyer, half-breed Crow Indian, Custer's chief scout.

ascertain in which direction the trail led; and if, as General Terry surmised, it led to the valley of the Little Big Horn, Custer was to follow the trail no further, but, sending scouts over it, he was to proceed south until he reached the headwaters of the Tongue, and there swing west and north, timing his marches to conform to the estimated progress of Gibbon's column, so that the two might reach the vicinity of the Little Big Horn valley at about the same time on the twenty-sixth, and so be in position to coöperate with each other in any fighting that might occur. And to Custer was detailed one of the best of Terry's scouts, George Herendeen, who was to be used as a courier to inform Terry, who had decided to march with Gibbon's column, of the movements of the Seventh, and its information of the enemy.

Unhappily, while there is no doubt as to his general scheme of operation, Terry's written instructions to Custer (Note 2) were not of a positive character; and Custer, for what cause and with what motive or reason no one can ever certainly know, did not carry through his commander's plan for coöperative action but, reaching the trail, at once followed it to the hostile camp, which he struck during the afternoon of June 25, in the valley of the Little Big Horn, about twenty miles from the mouth of that tortuous stream.

For nearly fifty years there has raged fierce and bitter controversy as to whether Custer wilfully disregarded Terry's instructions; and a strong case may be made out on either side the question. Since, however, it is not the purpose of this narrative to enter the field of controversy, but only to tell the story of the Seventh's crushing defeat at the hands of the Sioux, it is enough to state the fact that such dispute exists, and will, very likely, continue to exist so long as any of the men of the Old West survive.

Custer left the mouth of the Rosebud at noon, June 22, 1876, with twelve troops (or companies, as they were then called) of the Seventh Cavalry—the entire regiment, about six hundred strong, together with some forty Arikara (Ree) and Crow scouts, hereditary enemies of the Sioux Nation.

On the evening of June 24, the regiment bivouacked near where the station of Busby is now located, where it waited for intelligence from the friendly Indian scouts who had been sent on ahead.

Thus far, Custer's march from the mouth of the Rosebud had been conducted with the utmost precaution, and everything possible had been done to conceal the presence of the troops. All regimental divisions into wings and battalions had been abolished, the troop

[15]

commanders reporting to Custer in person. Bugle signals were forbidden, and the column marched so as to raise as little dust as possible, so that no lurking hostile warrior might detect the telltale signs of marching troops.

No one believed, when the Seventh left the mouth of the Rosebud on the twenty-second, no one had any reason to believe, that Sitting Bull's followers numbered in excess of a thousand to fifteen hundred warriors: indeed, estimates usually stopped far short of the smaller number; and there is abundant proof that Terry, as well as Gibbon and Custer, considered either column of the little army amply able to meet and defeat them. Terry's plan of combined operations was, however, directed rather to inclosing and capturing the Indians than to merely meeting and beating them in combat.

It was common belief that the Sioux would, upon the appearance of the troops, hasten to

A Seventh Cavalry group, taken during a hunting party in 1875. Left to right: Lt. James Calhoun; Leonard Swett of Chicago (civilian); Capt. Baker, 6th Inf.; Boston Custer; Lt. W. S. Edgerly; Miss Watson; Capt. Myles W. Keogh; Mrs. Calhoun; Mrs. Custer; General Custer; Dr. H. O. Paulding; Mrs. Algernon Smith; Dr. G. E. Lord; Capt. T. B. Weir; Lt. W. W. Cooke; Lt. Thompson, 6th Inf.; the Misses Wadsworth of Chicago; Capt. Thomas W. Custer; Lt. Algernon Smith. Of these, Calhoun, Boston Custer, Keogh, General Custer, Dr. Lord, Lt. Cooke, "Tom" Custer and Lt. Smith were killed at the Little Big Horn.

strike their camp and escape. Nobody entertained the thought that they would stand and fight a pitched battle. That was not the Indian way; nor had the troops heretofore found it possible to operate against them successfully otherwise than by surprise attacks. An hour's warning, and they were gone. Except in those rare instances when they had fallen upon some small, detached, and unfortunate band of soldiers, as in the Fetterman disaster of 1866, and by sheer force of numbers had annihilated it, the troops had found them more willing to run than to fight.

Custer had been unusually effective as an Indian fighter for several years. The greater part of his service since the close of the Civil War had been against Indians; he was an adept in bringing off surprise attacks that crushed and paralyzed resistance. Both his reputation and his experience as an Indian campaigner were second to none; and the

Seventh Cavalry, while its ranks were now full of recruits (Note 3), was held one of the best regiments in the service. It was but natural, then, that when the regiment marched proudly away from the mouth of the Rosebud on its mission, Terry could and did feel confident that if he could but catch the recalcitrant braves of Sitting Bull between Custer and Gibbon, he would certainly crush and capture them; and if, perchance, Custer found them elsewhere than was expected, the Seventh Cavalry, under such a leader, would be more than equal to any emergency.

Shortly after 9 P. M. of the twenty-fourth, the scouts reported to Custer that the trail of the Sioux led across the divide and into the valley of the Little Big Horn. He at once sent for his officers and, assembling them there in the darkness, told them what the scouts had found. He announced that the march of the regiment would be taken up at once, as he wished to get as nearly as possible to the divide before daybreak, when he would conceal the command during the day, locate definitely the Indian camp, and make his plans to attack it at dawn the day following, the twenty-sixth.

In the intense dark, progress was slow, and the command laboriously picked its way along, until at 2 A. M., June 25, having proceeded about ten miles toward the divide, the regiment again halted, to obtain further news from the scouts, who, under Lieutenant Varnum, had gone ahead to a high point on the divide known to the scouts as the Crow's Nest, from which one could see stretched out before him as in panorama, the valley of the Little Big Horn.

Varnum and his Indians reached the Crow's Nest before dawn; and as the first rays of sunlight illuminated the valley, the sharp eyes of the Indians detected, some fifteen miles away, immense herds of ponies that told them that the sleeping village of Sitting Bull was close at hand. Varnum at once sent word to Custer that the village had been located.

Custer received the message soon after daylight and ordered the regiment to move at eight o'clock. Shortly after that hour the command moved forward, slowly and cautiously, Custer himself hastening ahead to the Crow's Nest that he might confirm the report thus sent him by Varnum.

The regiment, having advanced within a short distance of the divide, again halted, and here Custer, returning from the lookout, once more called his officers together. He told them that the Indian scouts said the village was ahead, in the valley of the Little Big Horn; that he had not been able to see it himself, and doubted that it was there; but that "Mitch" Bouyer, the half-breed chief of scouts, had told him that he could see it

A Civil War portrait of Capt. F. W.
Benteen.

plainly, some fifteen miles down the valley. (Note 4.)

At this point two circumstances combined to compel Custer to abandon his expressed intention to lie in concealment during the day. Both incidents convinced him that the Sioux had discovered the presence of the command and that his only hope of success now lay in instant pursuit and immediate attack when he should come upon them.

During the night march one of the packs had become loosened, and a box of hard bread and a bag had dropped in the darkness somewhere along the trail. Sergeant Curtis of Yates's troop had been sent back, as soon as the loss was discovered, to pick up the missing articles before some watchful Sioux should find them. Going back some miles, he had indeed found the lost articles; but a small party of Sioux were before him, one of whom, when Curtis came upon them, was sitting upon the box and examining the contents of the bag. The Indians, upon sighting the sergeant, at once rode toward the valley. (Note 5.)

While Custer was on his way to the Crow's Nest, two or more Sioux scouts were discovered watching the command. They too had left in the direction of the village: and fresh pony tracks, found in a near-by ravine, indicated that a considerable party of warriors had been in close observation.

Further attempt at concealment was obviously useless. It was now near noon of the twenty-fifth, and Custer, all chance of surprise gone, and believing that the instant the Sioux scouts reached their village Sitting Bull and all his band would be on the move, scattering in all directions, led the regiment across the divide, to strike as soon as he could reach his wary enemy. Here, at 12:07 P. M., he halted, divided the regiment into battalions, and prepared for action.

II

LOOKING back upon what Custer did that day in June, 1876, in the light of all we knew now, it has seemed to many that he was reckless and foolhardy in the dispositions he made of his regiment. But it is neither just nor fair to judge his actions thus. The wisdom or unwisdom of his tactics must be determined, not in the light of what we know now, but of what he knew then, of the situation which confronted him.

In 1876 Montana was a wild, unsettled, and all but unexplored territory, in which there existed little or no means of communication. Telegraph lines were few and far between, and in the Rosebud country there were none. The telephone was as yet a thing unknown, and the only means available for the transmission of news was the mounted courier.

Custer did not know, nor did Terry and Gibbon know, that but the week before, at the very time when Reno was turning back to the north from his scout on the Rosebud, Crook was being met and checked by these same Sioux; that, led by Crazy Horse, and other famous war chiefs, the followers of Sitting Bull had held the Gray Fox, as Crook was called, and all but whipped him, not far from the place where Custer and his horsemen crossed the divide. They did not know that, flushed with success, Sitting Bull and his braves had been reinforced by hordes of young men from the reservations; that his camp held, not the thousand or fifteen hundred warriors that Terry and Gibbon and Custer expected to find and crush, but at least three times the larger number of fighting men. They did not know that the Indian agents had concealed the truth, if indeed they knew it, that a great part of the fighting strength of the Sioux Nation was with Sitting Bull; nor did they know that for many months the Indians had been acquiring from white traders repeating-rifles of the latest pattern, far superior to the ancient single-shot Springfield carbines carried by the troops; that they were possessed of ammunition in plenty, and were both prepared and determined to stand and fight.

Some inkling of these facts had indeed come to Sheridan after the expedition had taken the field, information that Sitting Bull's village contained some eighteen hundred lodges, which meant that there were with him from four to five thousand warriors; but there was no way to reach Terry except by courier. This Sheridan tried, but the fight was over long before the warning could arrive. (Note 6.)

When the regiment halted at 12:07 P. M., Custer, with his adjutant, Cooke, one of the most gallant soldiers of fortune that ever fought under the Stars and Stripes, withdrew a short distance from the command and with pencil and note-book divided the regiment into battalions, or, as we would call them now, squadrons. One squadron he assigned to Major Reno, the only field-officer, save himself, present with the regiment. This battalion consisted of Companies A, G, and M, under the commands of Captain Moylan, Lieutenant McIntosh, and Captain French, respectively. The second he gave to the senior captain, Frederick W. Benteen. This battalion comprised companies H, K, and D, which were commanded by Benteen, Lieutenant Godfrey, and Captain Weir. It is doubtful whether further battalion assignment was made, though it has been supposed that three companies were given to Captain Yates and two to Captain Keogh. The five companies which may have been so divided were C, E, F, I, and L. Of these, the first was commanded by General Custer's own brother, Captain Tom Custer; E, by Lieutenant Algernon Smith; F, by Captain Yates; I, by Captain Myles Keogh, and L, by Lieutenant Calhoun, Custer's brother-in-law. Whether battalion assignment of these five companies was in fact made is immaterial, since Custer retained them all under his personal command. B Company under Captain McDougall was assigned to the convoy of the pack-train, to which duty each of the other companies contributed one non-commissioned officer and six privates. Each of the latter was, assigned to lead two pack-mules.

At about 12:15 P. M., the battalion assignments having been completed, and all being ready for advance, Custer ordered Benteen with his battalion, approximately one hundred and twenty-five men in all, to proceed to the left, at an angle of about forty-five degrees from the route of the regiment, to scout the bluffs that loomed several miles distant; "to pitch into anything he might find," and report to Custer. Benteen at once took up his march, and within ten minutes, such was the broken nature of the terrain, was lost from view. Twice during the first few minutes of his march Custer sent him amendatory orders which directed him, in case he found nothing, to go on in the same direction to the valley beyond, and, if he still found nothing, to the next valley.

Benteen having departed, the rest of the regiment proceeded on its way, Reno with his battalion on the left bank of a small tributary of the Little Big Horn, and Custer with his five companies on the right bank. This tributary formed the middle branch of what is now known as Reno Creek.

It is well to keep in mind that when Benteen was sent off to the left the entire com-

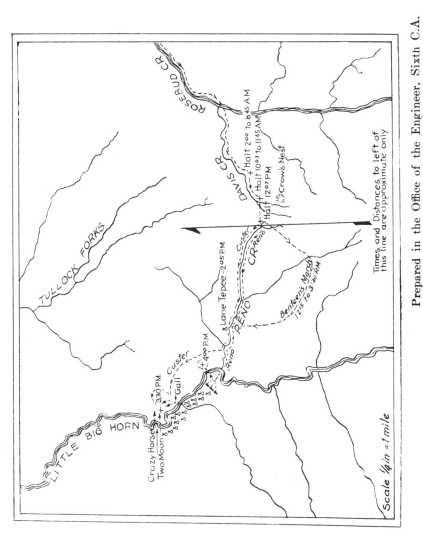

Map compiled by the author, showing the movements of the several detachments of the 7th Cavalry, June 25, 1876.

Prepared in the Office of the Engineer, Sixth C.A.

mand was nearly fifteen miles distant from where the Indian village, some two hours later, was found. This fact lends some color to the statements of Reno and Benteen, and of the scout Herendeen, afterward made and always persisted in, that Custer, when he crossed the divide and split up his regiment, was skeptical as to the location of an Indian village anywhere in that vicinity. (Note 4.)

Custer and Reno, following the opposite banks of the tributary, proceeded cautiously for about nine miles. Their lines of march were almost parallel; sometimes close together, sometimes as much as three hundred yards apart. At 2 P. M. Custer motioned with his hat for Reno to cross to the right bank, and the two columns then moved side by side, so close that the men freely conversed from one to the other.

Shortly after two o'clock a lone tepee was sighted. Custer immediately bore down upon it at a stiff trot. It proved to be the remnant of a freshly abandoned Indian village, all the tepees of which had been removed except this one, which was found to contain the dead body of a warrior. This "dead warrior tepee" was located on the south bank of the middle branch of the tributary now known as Reno Creek, and about three miles from its confluence with the Little Big Horn.

It was now about 2:15 P. M. As the command reached the tepee, which had been set afire by the Indian scouts who preceded the troops, a heavy dust-cloud was seen, apparently some five miles distant, across the river, and down the Little Big Horn valley. At the same moment, Fred Girard, a civilian interpreter, rode to the top of a small knoll, a short distance away, from which he saw a party of some forty Sioux between the troops and the river. They appeared to be in flight downstream.

Girard turned in his saddle and shouted to Custer, "Here are your Indians—running like devils." Instantly Custer ordered the Indian scouts ahead in pursuit, but they refused to go. To shame them he demanded that they give up their ponies and rifles, and turning to his adjutant, he gave the order that precipitated the action and proved fatal to the regiment.

Reno, at the head of his battalion, was just coming up. To him rode Cooke and said, "General Custer directs that you take as fast a gait as you deem prudent, and charge afterward, and you will be supported by the whole outfit."

When this order was given, Benteen with his battalion was probably eight to ten miles away to the left and rear. His position could at best be only approximated. It is certain, however, that he was not within coöperating distance, nor had his orders contemplated co-

[31]

operation with any other part of the regiment. When he was sent away, no village had been definitely located; no force of Indians had seen; and there neither was nor could have been at that time any definite plan, either of approach or of attack, in Custer's mind. It is important to remember this, for many if not most of those who have written of the battle of the Little Big Horn have assumed that Custer had made a definite plan of battle, in which Benteen's part was to attack the left flank of the village, Reno the front,. while Custer himself should come upon it from right and rear. But such assumptions are quite erroneous; there was no such plan, nor any plan, when Benteen was detached and sent away to explore the bluffs and valleys to the left. (Note 7.) Whatever scheme of attack was resolved upon was and must have been determined, if at all, more than two hours later and when Custer was some ten to twelve miles

Fred Gerard, the interpreter who pointed
out the fleeing Indians to Custer.

closer to the village: Benteen, at least, knew and could have known nothing of it.

The attack .order to Reno cannot be certainly reproduced. It was an oral order; and while it was heard by many who afterward tried to repeat it, there is disagreement in their accounts. Some say that the order directed Reno "to charge the Indians wherever you find them"; others, "to charge the village," or "charge afterward"; some, "to make for the dust." All accounts, however, agree as to the last phrase of the order, that Reno would be "supported by the whole outfit."

When the attack order was given, the village was not visible. Aside from the party of hostiles sighted by Girard as they fled down the river, no Indians were in sight. The one indication of any considerable force was the cloud of dust in the distance. Nothing had as yet developed to warn Custer that not a thousand, not fifteen hundred, but far nearer four thousand of the fiercest, bravest, most daring of savage warriors awaited him in the valley of the Little Big Horn: awaited him, elated by recent victory over Crook; armed with new repeating-rifles; literally loaded down with ammunition.

That little party of fleeing Indians, that cloud of dust in the valley, meant but one thing to Custer. The Sioux were running: and unquestionably in that belief he ordered Reno forward at rapid gait, to strike the enemy as hard and as quickly as he might. Nor is there any indication, much less any evidence, that Custer had then any other intention than to follow in Reno's tracks; to cross the river after him; to support his charge from the rear, and to hurl his five companies, a veritable thunderbolt, upon a startled, disorganized, and routed enemy.

Reno had three miles to go to the river. He made those three miles at a sharp trot, and crossed the river at about 2:30 P. M. Custer followed at a slower gait, being some three quarters of a mile behind when Reno's advance reached the stream. Cooke, the adjutant of the regiment, and Keogh, commander of I Company, rode to the river with Reno's column. There they turned back, to go to their deaths with Custer. (Note 8.)

All but five of the Indian scouts had gone with Reno. As they reached the stream, they excitedly pointed out to Girard, the interpreter who had first discovered the fleeing hostile party, that the Sioux had sighted Reno and were streaming up the valley to meet him. Girard, knowing that Custer believed the enemy in flight, galloped back on the trail, overtook Cooke, the adjutant, and told him that the Sioux were not running but were coming up the valley in heavy force. Cooke answered that he would at once report the fact to Custer, who up to that time was still following

[35]

Reno. Whether Cooke did so report, of course no man can say; but it must be assumed that he did, and within a very few minutes after 2:30 P. M.

Reno crossed the stream. In the fringe of woods upon the farther side he halted and reformed his command. Then, sending an orderly to Custer with the message that he had the enemy in force in his front, he trotted down the valley in line of battle, the Indian scouts under Varnum and Hare on his left front, A and M Companies in line, with G in reserve in the rear.

In this formation Reno's battalion swept towards the village, the first few tepees of which could now be seen through the shifting clouds of dust, some two miles down the river. Now G Company was called up on the line; and taking the gallop, the battalion rapidly neared its goal, Reno riding some twenty yards to front and center.

Lt. Charles A. Varnum, 7th Cavalry, in command of the "Ree" and Crow scouts at the Little Big Horn. He retired a Colonel and deceased in 1936, the last surviving officer who took part in the battle.

III

A S the battalion approached the village, out of the swirling clouds of dust stirred up by the Sioux to conceal their movements— an interesting forerunner of the smoke-screen made famous during the World War— mounted Indians, in what numbers no one could tell, could be seen dashing furiously about, now advancing, now circling, now receding, but all the time drawing the cavalry closer to the village. A few shots rang out to the left and front; the horses of the troopers, unused to so long a dash, were becoming excited and unruly, some of them getting entirely out of control. Suddenly the dust cleared, and Reno saw, in his front and to his left, mounted warriors by hundreds in

rapid motion. Again shots to the left, and
the Ree scouts scattered and vanished. Reno
halted; and as he did so, a large body of Indians swarmed from a ravine five hundred
yards away, menacing his left flank. Two of
his men, their horses frantic with excitement,
were carried into the Indian lines.

A heavily timbered bend of the river jutted
into the bed of the valley to his right; beyond
it flowed the rippling Little Big Horn River.
The nearest tepees of the village were still a
quarter of a mile away. Hundreds of yelling,
shooting Sioux were in his front; and other
hundreds were riding around his left flank,
which, no longer held by the Rees, was in the
air. He looked to the rear and looked again
for the promised support. It was not there.
Custer and his five companies had not followed him; and with every second, the
strength of the Sioux increased. Already
more warriors were opposed to his handful of

men, only 112 all told, than had been supposed the total of Sitting Bull's forces.

What to do! Should he continue his advance, charge forward into the village, and engulf his whole command in this swirling mass of savages, who, far from showing any signs of running, were rapidly and confidently attacking front and flank? Or should he take position and wait for supports? He must decide, and that instantly; and he did.

Reno has been bitterly criticized for what he did. He has been accused of cowardice; of disloyalty and wilful abandonment of his commander because he chose the latter course. Whether these accusations are justified, whether he, in the circumstances, did only what any sane leader would have done, must be left to the impartial verdict of history. He was not ordered to sacrifice his command, nor to ride headlong into an obvious trap, to inevitable annihilation. He halted, dismounted his men, and fought on foot, protecting his horses from the fire of the Indians by placing them in the timber. For a quarter of an hour, perhaps longer, his men, advancing until within three hundred yards of the southernmost tepees, stood off the Sioux, deployed in a thin blue line which stretched less than half-way across the valley, outnumbered ten to one, a hundred against a thousand. But the Indians were massing on his left and threatening his rear; they had begun to fire across the river from the east bank. Fearing, as he had every reason to fear, that, pursuing their usual tactics, the Sioux would now attempt to stampede his horses, which would be fatal to his command, he called G Company from its position on the line and placed it in the timber, A and M Companies extending to fill the gap by increasing their intervals. But now the line was too thin to hold the Sioux, and his unprotected left flank, upon which

This sketch of the Battlefield was made by a correspondent of the *New York Graphic* in July 1877 a little more than a year after the Battle. It was published with the caption: "Present appearance of the Little Big Horn Battle Field, Montana."

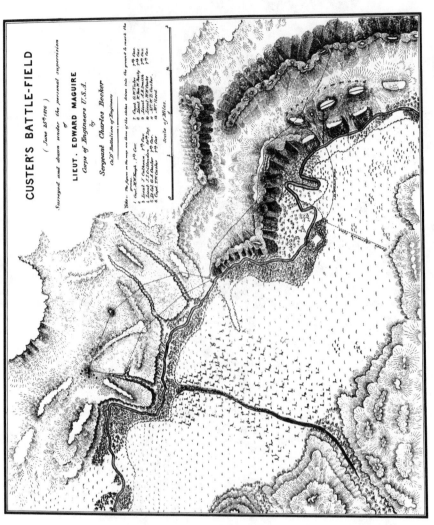

The battlefield map made by Lt. Maguire of the Engineers, June 28, 1876.

the pressure was over-great, was doubled back upon itself. His left was now completely turned, the two miles of valley between him and his crossing filled with Indians; the situation had become desperate. Twice before he halted he had sent messages to Custer to tell him that the Sioux were there in force; but no word had come from his chief since his order to attack was given. Once, indeed, just after the skirmish-line was formed, Lieutenant Wallace of G Company had tried to persuade a half-breed scout named Jackson to go to Custer with a call for help; but Jackson, waving his arm to the rear in the manner of Indians, refused. "No man could get through alive," he said. And no man could have done so then.

Reno now ordered his battalion to change front, and at the double the troops pivoted, to line the edge of the timber, a shift that put the timber and the river to the rear and the village on their right flank. Here they fought for half an hour or more; but they were too few to cover the position without getting beyond supporting distance of each other, and the Sioux were filtering through the woods to right and rear and were firing upon them from all sides. (Note 9.)

Up to this time Reno had lost but one man, Sergeant Heyn of A Company, who was shot through the breast as the skirmish-line made its change of front; but now bullets were flying among the horses, several of which were hit, the command was being surrounded by overwhelming numbers, and still no support had come. His ammunition was running low, and already the reserve in the saddle-bags and pockets had been drawn upon. A quick survey of the situation convinced Reno that he must get out; and more, that if he was to get out, he must do so quickly or remain there forever. He gave the order to get to the horses; but in the confusion many failed to hear or to understand it. A little clearing of about ten acres had been found in the center of the timber, which had evidently been the camping-ground of a Sioux medicine-man. It has been believed that this clearing was, in fact, the place where the tepees of Sitting Bull himself had stood; and in this clearing Reno formed his troops, the men leading in their mounts and standing to horse., (Note 9½)

Reno gave the command, "Mount." As he did so, a large party of Sioux broke through the timber and fired into the troops point-blank. At Reno's side fell the Ree scout Bloody Knife, shot through the head, his brains splashing into Reno's face and spattering his clothes. A trooper was mortally hit and with a fearful cry toppled from his saddle. Reno, startled and disconcerted, ordered the men to dismount and to mount again, and whirling his horse, broke through the timber

[43]

and so out upon the plain, closely followed by the confused troopers. Here they hastily formed an irregular column, and at the gallop, led by Reno, started up the valley toward the ford at which they had crossed in their advance. Seventeen men were left behind in the woods; among them Lieutenant De Rudio, Private O'Neil of G Company, Girard the interpreter, and the half-breed Jackson. (Note 20, paragraph 4.) The famous scout Charley Reynolds, who had remained behind in the timber when the troops rode out, dashed to overtake them and was met by an Indian bullet which stretched him dead upon the plain. McIntosh, commander of G Company, which was scattered through the woods when the order to leave was given, strove to rally and collect his men, few of whom had heard the order. At the edge of the timber his horse went down, an arrow through its head. Back into the woods he darted, where

"Lonesome Charley" Reynolds, a famous scout.
Killed during Reno's retreat.

a trooper of G Company gave up his mount to his officer. Again McIntosh left the woods, now far behind the command. The Sioux rode between, and he died.

The column, led by Reno, with pistols drawn, charged into the horde of Indians, which gave way to let the soldiers pass, and instantly closed in. The pressure from the right was too strong, the weight too heavy; and Reno, realizing that he could not cut through to the ford at which he crossed, swerved to the left and so struck the river more than a mile to the north, down-stream, from the point of his first crossing.

The head of the column reached the river in fair order, the horses at the run. Few if any Indians had been encountered to the left; but to the right of the column there were hundreds, who raced along parallel with the troops, pumping their new Winchesters as fast as they could load and fire, ducking behind the

shoulders of their agile ponies whenever a
trooper raised his pistol. The charge quickly
became retreat at the head of the column, rout
at the center, panic at the rear. All along the
route to the river men and horses dropped.
It was a hand-to-hand combat for the rearmost
troopers all the way. Lieutenant Varnum,
left behind at the start, raced his horse to the
front, shouting, "For God's sake, men, don't
run; we've got to go back and save the
wounded." But he could not stop them.

At the river-bank a sheer drop of six feet to
the water below checked the foremost horses,
many of which refused to jump. The pressure from those behind forced them over the
crumbling bank, and down they went, men
and horses floundering together in the water,
at that point four feet deep. It was each man
for himself now, and no one thought to stop,
to make any attempt to protect the crossing
for the others, or to resist the frenzied Sioux,

who from the banks above and below, from both sides of the stream, poured a steady fusillade of bullets into the jammed and panic-stricken troops. Twenty-nine of the 112 were killed and many wounded before the crossing was negotiated.

Benny Hodgson, Reno's adjutant, pet and favorite of the regiment, was hit as his horse took the jump. The bullet tore through his thigh and killed his horse, which sank under him in the river. Struggling to his feet, he seized the stirrup-strap of a passing trooper and was dragged through the water to the other side. The trooper tried to raise him to his horse but failed; and Hodgson, unable to use his leg, faced the Indians, pistol in hand. An instant later he was shot down and died, nobly, upon the river-bank. De Wolf, the surgeon, crossed in safety and with his orderly, Clair of K Company, coolly started up a ravine to the left. They had gone but a few yards when both were shot down and scalped by painted warriors in plain view of the fleeing troopers.

At the place of Reno's crossing in retreat, the right bank rises abruptly to hills that tower above the stream. The panting men and horses struggled up the rise, and there Varnum, having now stopped the flight of the leaders, was reforming them when Reno, hatless, excited, and out of breath, reached the top. As the scattered remnants of his three troops, some wounded, many without mounts, all discomfited and disorganized, were gathered together, they were posted hastily to fend off the expected rush of the Sioux.

Thus ended the first phase of the battle of the Little Big Horn. Reno had crossed the river to the attack about 2:30 P. M. His halt to re-form in the timber on the left bank could not have taken less than ten minutes; and it was not earlier than three o'clock when, after his advance down the valley, his forward movement was checked. His action in the valley lasted the better part of three quarters of an hour, and it was after four o'clock when, routed and disorganized, and almost out of ammunition, his command reached the hills upon the right bank, having lost in killed and wounded and missing nearly half of the battalion.

Had the Sioux followed him across the river in attack, as he had every reason to apprehend they would do, there can be no question that his command would have been as completely obliterated as was Custer's later in the day. Many of the warriors did, in fact, ford the river above the command, and were advancing up the slopes and ravines to intercept the retreat when the attention of the greater part of the Indian force was for the time diverted to another part of the fatal field.

Lt. W. W. Cooke, Adjutant of the 7th Cavalry, who at Custer's direction wrote the famous last message to Benteen to "Come on. Big Village. Be quick. Bring packs."

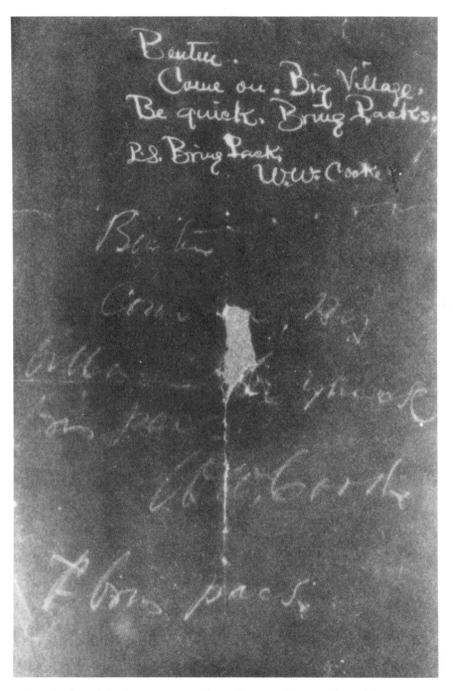

Reproduction of the famous message from Custer to Benteen. The original was presented to Colonel Benteen in 1879 to Captain Robert Newton Price and is now in the Library at West Point.

IV

WHERE during all this time was Custer; and where Benteen? The question was in the mind and upon the lips of every man of Reno's stricken battalion, as it crouched apprehensive on that hill, hoping, praying for aid, expecting every instant to find the Sioux again upon it.

Benteen, ordered to scout the bluffs and valleys to the left, had diverged from the route of the regiment soon after the halt at 12:07 P. M., when the division into battalions was made. No one had seen him since, nor knew his whereabouts or doings. Whether he too had fought an action no one knew. Ten minutes after his departure the bad lands had swallowed him, as completely as if he had gone into the bowels of the earth.

Carrying out Custer's orders, Benteen had taken a fast walk, sending Lieutenant Gibson and a squad of ten in advance of the battalion. With his orderly trumpeter alone, he much of the time rode far to the front, preceding even his own scouts. He reached the bluffs, some four miles distant from where he had left the regiment, and sent Gibson to the top. No Indians in sight; nothing in sight but more bluffs; no sign of a valley as far as eye could see. The ground was very rough and cut with innumerable gullies and ravines; bad lands of the most rugged type, almost impassable for anything but goats. Now skirting the bluffs for several miles, he sent Gibson to the top time after time, but always the signal came back, "No enemy in sight." (Note 10.) He was satisfied that nothing was to be found in this direction, and that even Indians would never cross a country such as this unless they could find no other path. He felt that Custer's orders had been ill considered, that his march was a waste of time and effort and had sent beyond hope of coöperation three full companies which might be sorely needed in the fight which he believed was sure to come on the trail the rest of the regiment had followed. (Note 11.)

Having satisfied himself, therefore, after marching some twelve miles, that he could accomplish nothing where he was, he took the bit in his teeth, and, disregarding orders further, turned toward the direction in which the regiment was headed when he left it, and, at about the same angle to the trail, hurried to overtake the other battalions. His march had covered some fifteen miles, all to the left and rear of the command, when he again struck into the trail. It was now near the middle of the afternoon, probably about 3:30.

As he reached the trail, he stopped at a boggy morass to water his horses, which were weary and hot with their three hours of climbing and sliding in the bad lands; and here Captain Weir of D Company, hearing some distant shots, became impatient and took the lead without orders. As Benteen left the morass, the first mules of the pack-train appeared, and these, frantic with thirst, rushed into the bog and mired down. Two miles further on he came to the lone tepee, from which nearly two hours before Girard had first sighted the fleeing band of Indians, and from which, at the same time, the dust-cloud in the valley had been seen by the regiment. A mile beyond the tepee, Sergeant Kanipe of C Company, Tom Custer's troop, arrived with an order to the commanding officer of the pack-train to "hurry up the packs." Telling the sergeant that the train was following far to the rear, he pointed out the direction, and rode on. A mile or so further and he was met by another messenger, a member of his own troop. This was John Martin, who had been detailed as Custer's orderly trumpeter that day. Martin was a green Italian lad who, born Giovanni Martini, had served under Garibaldi as a drummer-boy at Villafranca. He had been but a year in America and spoke and understood but little English. Martin bore Custer's last message, written and signed by his adjutant, which read: "Benteen—Come on —Big Village—Be quick—Bring packs." And after Cooke had scrawled his signature, he had added hurriedly, "P. S. Bring pacs." (Note 12.)

Benteen received this message sometime near four o'clock, after he had proceeded, following the trail of the regiment, for about three miles beyond the "dead warrior tepee." It seems likely that he had taken Custer's trail rather than Reno's, since three miles from the tepee on Reno's trail would have brought him almost to the river. Custer, however, after following Reno for more than two miles after leaving the tepee, struck off sharply to the right down-stream. As Martin had followed Custer's route back, he probably met Benteen on Custer's trail, approximately a mile south of the hill on which Reno took refuge after his disastrous action in the valley and subsequent crossing of the river.

Martin had been fired upon by the Sioux as he made his perilous ride to Benteen; his horse had been struck and was bleeding profusely, the animal being at the point of exhaustion when he arrived. He had seen Reno in action in the valley and was jubilant and elated, telling Benteen that the Indians were "skedaddling," that Custer was charging through the village. During his ride back he had met Boston Custer, the youngest of the general's brothers, who had accompanied the expedition as a civilian forage-master. Young Custer had, for some reason, left the general's column and returned to the pack-train on an errand, and was riding furiously to overtake the fated five companies, which were even then turning toward the ridge where they perished to a man one short hour later.

Benteen read the message carried by the excited Martin, showed it to Weir and Edgerly, the officers of D Company, as they rode up; and then, quickening the pace, he rode to the sound of the guns that could now be heard distinctly in the valley below. He did not pause to bring up the packs; he had sent Sergeant Kanipe to the train commander with Custer's order to hurry. Leading his battalion, he went forward.

Coming to a rise in the ground, the valley of the Little Big Horn opened before him; and there, in the dust and smoke, Benteen's command saw that which must for the moment have dismayed them. An overwhelming force of yelling, painted Sioux, sweeping and

From the Briminstool collection.

An artist's conception of Custer's last stand: original in Karl May Museum, Dresden. While not so well known as the famous Anheuser-Busch advertising picture, it is probably more nearly accurate.

Courtesy of the Custer Battlefield National Monument, National Park Service

John Martin, born Giovanni Martini, the trumpeter who, as General Custer's orderly, bore his last message to Benteen— "Come on—big village—be quick—bring packs."

swooping from all directions, were riding down and killing a little band of soldiers who were vainly trying to reach the river. It was the last of Reno's command, those who had been unhorsed and left behind during the mad rush for the bluffs.

As Benteen and his battalion appeared over the crest of the ridge, the Indians sighted them and immediately opened fire, their bullets striking all about and at the feet of the horses. The range was too long, however, to do them any damage. Undecided what to do, Benteen was considering the crossing of the river, when he saw, some hundreds of yards to his right, a party of Indians. Lieutenant Godfrey of K Company rode swiftly toward them and found them to be a group of the Crow scouts, among whom was their leader, Half Yellow Face, who motioned him to continue to the right. As the command neared the Crows, Lieutenant Godfrey rode to Half Yellow Face, pointed to the valley and then to the hills, and asked, "Soldiers?" The Crow shook his head and, sweeping his arm to the right, answered, "Soldiers," at the same time pointing out the hill to which Reno had fled.

Benteen's battalion drew pistols and trotted forward. As they approached the hill, Reno, dismounted and with his head tied with a handkerchief, ran breathless out to meet them. "For God's sake, Benteen," he shouted, "halt your command and help me. I've lost half my men." A minute later and Benteen's battalion had joined the remnants of Reno's on the top of the hill. Reno, his overwrought nerves still in the ascendant, his self-control gone, broke off in the midst of a sentence to fire a revolver at the Indians a thousand yards away. Even Varnum, hero though he had proved himself that day, was beside himself, both with rage against the Sioux and with grief over the death of Hodgson, his dearest friend. He too seized a carbine and commenced to fire at the distant enemy.

The whole of Reno's command was disorganized, excited, and on edge. A few, however, through all the harrowing experience, had remained cool and self-possessed. Some of the rearmost who had escaped the Sioux were still coming up the bluff, one man nonchalantly waving a scalp freshly ripped from the head of an Indian warrior. Lieutenant Hare, Godfrey's subaltern in K Company, who with Varnum had been in charge of the scouts who rode with Reno, enthusiastically shook the hand of his troop commander, saying with much gusto: "I'm damned glad to see you. We had a big fight in the valley and got whipped like hell." His laconic description stated the situation exactly.

Upon Benteen's arrival it was he, not Reno, who was the real commanding officer. Benteen was a man of magnificent presence and dominating personality; cool, keen, daring, and brave as a lion; and he quickly brought order out of confusion. His troops were ordered at once to divide their ammunition with Reno's men, who had almost exhausted their own during the fight in the valley. Reno's companies were re-formed, and the combined battalions placed in a proper attitude of defense. Lieutenant Hare, impressed by Reno as battalion adjutant in place of the unfortunate Hodgson, was despatched on the freshest horse to be found, to ride at top speed to the pack-train, whose dust could be seen in the distance, with orders to cut out and rush forward the ammunition-mules and to hasten the progress of the train. Hare's company commander, Godfrey, gave up his own mount that the perilous ride might be made. In the meantime the command made ready for any eventuality. They were no longer menaced by the Sioux, the greater part of whom had left their front and had ridden pell-mell down the valley. Only a few now remained to watch and harass them with long-distance fire.

V

WHILE the last of Reno's men were arriving on the hill immediately after Benteen's arrival, firing, heavy and continuous, had been heard. It came from downriver Some one was fighting there, and furiously. The Indians opposed to Reno had heard it too and had ridden by hundreds in that direction. (Note 13.)

Benteen had shown Custer's message to Reno immediately upon joining him. He had asked Reno as to Custer's whereabouts. Reno did not know, nor did any of his command: no word of any kind had come from their chief since the attack order at 2:15, and it was now near 4:30. More than two hours had elapsed since they had parted at the lone tepee. Custer had not crossed the river at the southern end of the village; that was certain. He had not gone back toward the packs; that also was certain. He must be to the north, down-stream, for Martin had come from that direction. It was surely Custer who was engaging the Indians below.

As they listened and wondered on the hill, two distant volleys rang out. Weir, commander of D Company, sprang to his feet, exclaiming to his lieutenant, Edgerly, "That's Custer."

"Yes," Edgerly replied, "and we ought to go down there."

Weir thought a moment. "I'm going to ask them; but if they won't take the command, are you willing to go with D Company alone?"

"Yes," said Edgerly, "I am." Weir strode away. He spoke heatedly with Reno; then, alone but for his orderly, he rode to the north.

Edgerly, supposing that permission had been given, followed with the company. They advanced a mile or more down-stream until from a high point they could see the Indians, some of whom were gathered in groups, while others rode about, shooting at objects on the ground. But no engagement was in progress. Whatever of combat there had been was finished now; and if the sounds of battle they had heard, the volleys that had reached their ears, had indeed come from Custer it was evident that he was no longer fighting there.

Weir and his troop, searching out that field with straining eyes, wondered what had become of their commander. Little did they imagine the truth. Nor did any member of Reno's command, which soon followed Weir's advance, draw any other inference from what they dimly saw in the distance than that Custer had found the Sioux too strong and, repulsed, had gone to join forces with the advancing columns of Terry. They had but to hold their own yet a little while and Custer would come charging back again with reinforcements. (Note 14.)

Reno had waited for the pack-train to come up before he followed Weir's advance and was now well stocked with ammunition. The train had been slow in arriving, and it was after five o'clock before the last mules were up. He had many wounded to carry. He could not leave them behind, and it took six men to carry one. Progress was slow. His advance, led by Benteen, reached Weir close to six o'clock, when it took position on the hills and faced the approaching Sioux, who now were swarming up the gorge to attack.

Soon the leading companies were engaged; and Reno and Benteen, quickly surveying the field, decided that this was no place to stand and fight, since stand and fight they must.

[65]

Orders were given to retire to the hill whence they had just come; and the command now slowly retraced its steps, each company as it arrived on the hill being placed by Benteen. K, Godfrey's company, was the last to reach the position, having covered the last lap of the retreat; and as the dismounted troopers, close to seven o'clock, made the final dash to the rear, the battle was on.

The Sioux attack followed the troops closely. Reno was immediately surrounded and besieged, fighting with desperation until merciful darkness, settling down upon the hills, made it impossible longer to see. Not until then did the vengeful warriors withdraw, having killed and wounded many of the little band upon the hill, and played havoc among the unprotected animals.

That night, in the Indian village across the Little Big Horn, there was revelry and celebration. That night, among the little band of soldiers on the hill, there was feverish preparation for defense against the attack that all knew would be renewed with the first blush of daylight; and many were the muttered curses, both of officer and man, that Custer and his five companies had deserted them.

All night long the little band burrowed in the dusty, flinty ground, scooping out, with such implements as they could improvise—for three spades and two axes were the only tools they possessed—shallow holes which would afford some cover. Working, perforce, with knives and spoons, all except Benteen's company dug in as best they might. During the night, positions hastily taken the evening before were revised; gaps in the line were closed; the animals were picketed and protected as much as the terrain would permit. The line girded the hill below its crest in an oval formation, the animals being placed in a depression near the center, which was shielded from the fire of the Indians in all directions save the east. Reno, with McDougall (B), Wallace (with the remnant of G), French (M), Godfrey (K), and Weir (D), held the northerly curve of the oval; Moylan, with A, the eastern side; and Benteen, with H, the south. The western side of the oval had natural protection in the steep slope to the river, which could be swept by cross-fire from north and south. Bread-boxes, saddles, everything that would stop a bullet or an arrow were piled in front of the shallow holes; ammunition was distributed; and the command was ready, grimly awaiting the onslaught of the savage enemy.

Two o'clock. Darkness, heavy, impenetrable, still hung over the hills. The Indian village was still and quiet. Scouts who had ventured forth returned to say that no sign of Custer could be found, and the country around about was full of Indians. Two-thirty, and the faint dawn that precedes the sunrise began

"Curley," a Crow Indian scout, long believed to be a
survivor of Custer's battalion.

to lighten the hilltops. Day comes in the mountains as swiftly as the night falls: a few minutes now, and the tale would be told. Silently the men, who had snatched a few minutes of sleep, were wakened; as silently each one crept to his appointed place; the defense was ready, peering out into the quickly lifting murk for the unseen foe.

Two forty-five. The hilltops were light, the valley below visible through the mist. And now a single rifle-shot rang out, followed at a short interval by another. It was the enemy's signal, and upon the instant there poured from all directions, from every vantage-point that could conceal a warrior, the crashing fire of the Sioux, which steadily increased in volume as broad daylight cleared the scene of action.

Following the time-honored tactics of the Indian, the warriors fired from cover, for the most part at will, though frequently in regular and ordered volleys. To draw the fire of the troops they resorted to every stratagem known to the savage mind; now standing erect for an instant, then dropping from sight; raising hats or other head-gear above the bush. But these devices did not serve, for except a few picked shots the men were forbidden to return the fire.

During the fiercest of the fighting and once during the night of the twenty-fifth bugle-calls were heard by the hard-pressed soldiers. Some, believing relief at hand, anxiously scanned the hills for signs of Custer's column. Others, all hope of reinforcement long since gone, were now convinced that white allies were arrayed against them with the Indians. But no relieving column came, and here and there, as the wary foe exposed himself, they glimpsed for the instant men clad in white men's garb; some, indeed, in the uniform of the army. A cry went round the hill: "Deserters are with them! White renegades are fighting with the Sioux!" Not till long afterward was the truth revealed: that Indian braves had stripped clothing from Custer's dead, soldiers and civilians alike, and had donned it in an attempt to lure Reno's men from their secure position; that the bugle, torn from the body of some ill-fated trumpeter of Custer's battalion, had been sounded by an Indian warrior with the same crafty purpose. (Note 15.)

Benteen's company, exposed to fire from the rear, suffered more than the others. His was the weakest spot in the line as well as the key to the position. Sensing this, the Sioux concentrated upon him a heavy force, which, while keeping up a steady fusillade, crept ever nearer. He left the company to go over the crest to Reno to demand reinforcement, which Reno reluctantly gave, sending Captain French with M Company to his aid. During the few minutes of Benteen's absence, one daring warrior crept close enough to count coup on the body of a soldier that lay within his lines.

The situation had become both critical and desperate; and Benteen, thinking attack the best defense, charged the Indians, scattering them from his front. To Reno now he went, urging that he too must drive the Sioux from that front also or be overwhelmed. Reno, loath to risk further losses, hesitated. But Benteen insisted and insisted again, until Reno, lying flat upon the ground at Benteen's feet, told him that if he could see the Indians, to give the order.

During all the fight upon the hill Benteen had shown extraordinary courage and the utmost disdain of the Sioux. He exposed himself freely, walking about with a smile upon his face, his white hair, like Navarre's plume, shining in the sun. With words of cheer and

[72]

encouragement to the men worth more than reinforcement, his example inspired them all to deeds of heroism. He gave the order: "Ready, men!—Now!—Charge and give them hell!" Led by Reno, the four companies dashed forward just in time to scatter a large body of warriors who were gathering for a rush. Then back they raced to their shallow defenses. Not a man had been lost in the sortie.

As the sun mounted high in the heavens, the heat became intense, and the suffering from want of water, of which there had been none for nearly twenty-four hours, became unendurable. Volunteers crept down to the river, a quarter of a mile away, carrying with them canteens and kettles; and thus, though at heavy risk, a few swallows of the life-giving fluid were obtained for the wounded and the thirst-maddened men.

Shortly after midday, Sioux scouts rode into

the village from down the valley, and there ensued much talking and powwowing among the chiefs. Soon the squaws began to dismantle the tepees; and the braves, at the signal of their leaders, withdrew by sections, a few score at a time, until, when the entire village had been torn down, the pony herds gathered, the squaws and children collected, the last of the warriors left the hill and late in the afternoon joined the moving village, which slowly made its way, in precise formation, toward the Big Horn Mountains.

Freed now from the terrors of the past two days, Reno's men watched them depart; and though they knew not why deliverance had come, they thanked God for it. They had suffered heavily. Eighteen men had been killed on the hill, and fifty-two wounded; and the loss of animals, exposed as they were to long-range fire, had been terrible.

THE LITTLE BIG HORN

A group of officers gathered on the high ridge near the river to watch the Indians depart. Not until then had they been able to form any real estimate of the strength of the Sioux. The moving village, which remained in sight for several hours, bulked against the setting sun as a solid mass of savages and animals, as numerous and as precisely organized as a division of cavalry on the march. The number of ponies was variously estimated as between fifteen and twenty-five thousand, and the fighting strength of the village, exclusive of the hundreds of women and children, from three to five thousand. It was the largest gathering of Indians ever seen upon the plains. The standing village, as was afterward determined, had been placed along the west bank of the Little Big Horn, each of the various tribes camping by itself. From one end to the other, it covered a distance of nearly four

[75]

miles and was at some points nearly half a
mile in depth. More than fifteen hundred
lodges had been erected and occupied, besides
innumerable wickiups.

Safe for the time but in bad case, Reno's
men had now time to think and to relax.
During the early evening the dead on the hill
were buried, the bodies of those who fell on
the east bank during the retreat from the valley were recovered, and the position was
shifted, both to be nearer water and to escape
from the stench of dead animals upon the hill.

Then came discussion and debate. What
had become of Custer? Why had he left
them to their fate? For what reason had he
deserted them? Had he ridden north to join
with Terry, or had he turned to the south in
search of Crook? It was not like Custer to
allow an enemy to escape; yet the enemy had
escaped, and Custer was not there. Why did
he not come? What could he be doing?

"Comanche." The only real survivor of Custer's last fight.

Courtesy of the Custer Battlefield National Monument, National Park Service

Photo by Brininstool.

The valley of the Little Big Horn. The Sioux village extended for several miles along the farther bank of the river. This view taken from Reno Hill.

Courtesy of the Custer Battlefield National Monument, National Park Service

THE LITTLE BIG HORN

And thus throughout the night ran comment
and conjecture, sometimes not over-kind to
the absent commander and his five companies
of their comrades-in-arms.

VI

WHAT indeed had become of Custer; and what of the gallant 225 who rode with him?

During the morning of the twenty-sixth, Terry's scouts, led by Lieutenant James H. Bradley of the Seventh Infantry, pushed ahead of Gibbon's plodding column under urgent instructions from General Terry to get in touch with the Seventh Cavalry. They came upon some Indians, who fled across the Big Horn on their approach, leaving on the bank clothing that was recognized as a part of that worn by the Crow scouts who had left the Yellowstone with Custer. They were induced to return only when satisfied that Bradley and his party were not of the dreaded Sioux.

To these they told a tale of battle and destruction. They said that Custer had met the Sioux, that he and hundreds with him had been killed; the survivors were besieged and in dire distress.

A messenger from Bradley galloped posthaste to the rear and to Terry reported what the Crows had said. The story was not credited. That disaster of such proportions could have overtaken such a regiment as the Seventh Cavalry was preposterous. Yet since fighting must have occurred, Terry urged the column forward, and at nightfall the exhausted doughboys camped in the Little Big Horn valley, some nine miles below the scene of Reno's siege. During the latter part of the day's march the Sioux in heavy force were in their front; and it is known that this approach of Gibbon's column on the twenty-sixth was all that caused the Indians to abandon their effort to wipe out Reno's command.

At daybreak on the twenty-seventh, Bradley and his scouts were again in motion up the river, taking the hills on the eastern side, while Terry, with Gibbon's command, marched up the valley.

Soon after crossing the river, Bradley and his party came to a point from which they saw, lying there in the glare of the morning sun, objects which gleamed white in the distance. As they drew nearer, confirmation both horrible and shocking proved the accuracy of the story told by the frightened Crows.

On the field before him, cold in death, lay the bodies of more than two hundred white men, and, about them and among them, the carcasses of many horses. There was no doubt now that the Crows had told the truth.

Again Bradley sent the word to Terry, who at the head of Gibbon's little command was hurrying up the valley. To him was borne

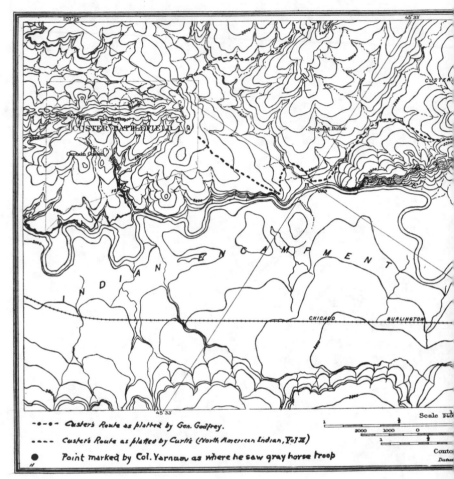

- -o- -o- -o- Custer's Route as platted by Gen. Godfrey.
- - - - Custer's Route as platted by Curtis (North American Indian, Vol. III)
● Point marked by Col. Varnum as where he saw gray horse troop

Contour map of the battlefield. (U. S. Geologic

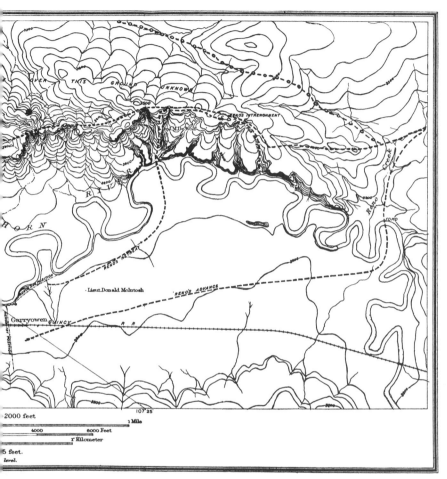

uster's route as supposed by Curtis and Godfrey.

the solemn news and to him related the evidence that his scouts had seen.

From the heights overlooking the valley of their tribulation, the survivors of Reno's command saw the approach of the little column. Whether it was friend or foe they could not tell. But as they watched the slow, methodical advance, it gradually took form. Unless the Sioux were imitating soldiers, the formations were those of troops. Reno ordered Lieutenants Wallace and Hare to cross the river and to ascertain who and what the column was.

Quickly they mounted horses and were on the way. A few minutes' gallop and the infantry and cavalry of Gibbon's command loomed near enough to prove relief at hand. Putting spur to the horses, they dashed ahead, and as they reined beside General Terry, from the lips of both came the same questions:

"Where is Custer? Have you seen him? Why is he not with you?"

When General Terry and his staff arrived upon the hill where Reno and his beleagured men awaited him, among the rescued men both joy and grief struggled for the mastery. Strong men wept unashamed, while rejoicing at their own deliverance. All were shaken to the depths of their souls over the appalling news of Custer's fate, of which no man of Reno's command had entertained the least suspicion.

That afternoon, Benteen, accompanied by a party of officers was led by Bradley to the scene of Custer's last fight. What they found there—what they saw—is all that ever has been known, all that ever will be known of the manner of his fate; for save such tales as were long afterward wrung from unwilling members of the Indian horde that snuffed him out, and with him every officer and soldier of his command, no witness to the tragedy was ever found. The evidence of the stricken field alone remained to bear mute testimony of a gallant, desperate combat to the death. One living thing they found upon that field,—one only; the horse "Comanche," Keogh's mount.

No one knows certainly to this day what route Custer took after leaving Reno's trail. No one knows why he changed his plan to follow Reno in support. The only ones who knew died with him.

Part of the way—part only—can we follow him and his devoted band; after that, the trail is closed.

Shortly after turning to the north, he despatched Sergeant Kanipe of C Company with an order addressed to the commanding officer of the train. It bade him "hurry up the packs." That order, as has been before related, the sergeant had delivered to Benteen, who sent him on his way to find the train.

After Kanipe had left the column, it proceeded north at a gallop for more than a mile, when Custer, having already sent "Mitch" Bouyer and the four Crow scouts who remained with him to the ridge, halted the command under the shadow of a towering hill. Accompanied by his brother and the adjutant, and by his nephew "Autie" Reed, the general galloped to the crest of the ridge to look down upon the village. At least one enlisted man went with him, John Martin of H Company, his orderly trumpeter.

Sharply the general scanned the valley with ready glasses. The village seemed asleep. Save for a few dogs and ponies, lazy in the sun, a few squaws and romping children were all that could be seen. The camp was lifeless, apparently denuded of fighting men.

Abruptly he turned to his companions. "We 've got them," he exclaimed. "We 've caught them napping. Come on!" And wheeling his horse, with a wave of his hat to the waiting troops, he dashed back to the command and, with a cheer, again led them to the north.

A mile further on they went, trotting, galloping, all the way, the intervening hills screening them from the village. Then the general, turning to his orderly, said: "I want you to take a message to Captain Benteen. Ride fast as you can and tell him to hurry. Tell him it 's a big village, and I want him to be quick, and to bring the ammunition-packs."

Martin checked his horse and was turning when the adjutant cried, "Wait, orderly; I 'll give you a message," and tore from his book the note which reached Benteen at Martin's hands, some three miles from the lone tepee. When Martin left the column, it was turning toward the river. He was the last man to see Custer alive, except those who rode on, and perished on the ridge. (Note 12.)

It is known that somewhere between the point where Kanipe left the column and where Martin turned back with Custer's last message, one set of fours dropped out, their horses exhausted. Two at least of these men, Privates Thompson and Watson, both of C Company, joined Reno later in the day. The others were probably killed by the Indians.

So far we can follow Custer and his men on their ride to death. Little more is known. The accounts given by the Sioux differ so widely that little satisfactory information can be culled from them. Their stories cannot be reconciled. The field of battle, however, proved that Custer had ridden down the river some five miles from the point at which he diverged from Reno's trail, evidently with intent to strike the Indian village in flank or rear. Whether he attempted to cross the river is unknown; but the fact that several headless bodies of his men were found in the

Photo by Brininstool.

Where Custer made his last stand.

village, nearly opposite the scene of his destruction, would seem to indicate that some of his men may have penetrated the village. But whether in attack or in attempted flight, it is impossible even to conjecture.

It is probable that he approached the village from the southeast, emerging from behind the hills and ridges that screened the march of his troops until he turned toward the river, and that he was attacked and overwhelmed before he had time or opportunity to strike the village, which lay on the other side. It was apparent that the brunt of the Sioux attack came from the south, that Calhoun's troop was the first to be struck by the savage mass, and, immediately after, Keogh's. Aside from these two troops, in which officers and men died in their places, in platoon formation, there was no semblance of battle-lines anywhere on the field. All was confusion. The tide of battle had swept over Calhoun and Keogh, crushing them by sheer weight of numbers, and, rolling onward, had first enveloped, then engulfed, the other three companies. The great war chief Gall of the Hunkpapás led the main attack, which broke the troop formations and pushed the swirling, fighting, milling mass to the north, until, upon the ridge where now stands the battle monument, assailed in the rear by the Ogalallas under Crazy Horse and Two Moon's fierce Cheyennes, both flanks turned, enveloped by overwhelming numbers on every side and swept with fire from every direction, the gallant Custer and his comrades fell. To the thousands that attacked him as he approached the river, there were added, during the later moments of the struggle, hundreds of warriors fresh from Reno's rout, in headlong charge.

That the combat was intense, that soldier and officer alike sold his life as dearly as he might, there is no doubt. At the point on the

Photo by Barry.

"Gall." the Hunkpapa war chief, who, after routing Reno, rode to the attack on Custer and led the charge that exterminated his command.

ridge where lay the bodies of the slain leader and his officers, all save those of Keogh's and Calhoun's troops, there was ample evidence that the final struggle was terrible in its desperation. Horses and men lay thick about the body of the general, who, shot through the temple and the left breast, had sunk to death between the corpses of two of his men, his arms, outstretched, resting across the bodies. Only a few feet away lay the mutilated remains of the general's brother, Tom, the captain of C Troop, while Yates and Smith, Reilly and Cooke were close at hand. Grouped around their officers were found the bodies of some two score soldiers who had rallied to support their general's last stand. And for a mile square the field was dotted with the corpses of the slain, some in little groups, some alone and separated from the others by many yards. Of the 225 officers and men who rode with Custer into the fight that day, not one was left alive. They were wiped out, obliterated, exterminated to a man. The Indian loss was negligible. (Note 15½.)

The Battle Monument.

VII

AND so ended the battle of the Little Big Horn. Upon the fatal field where Custer and his five companies fought and fell there were recovered more than two hundred bodies; and these, with few exceptions, were buried where they lay, in shallow graves. Some were never accounted for; but from that day to this, no trace of a single survivor has ever been found. They were utterly exterminated; not one escaped the fury of the Sioux. Even Thermopylæ spared one. (Note 16.)

Reno's losses during his fighting in the valley, along the course of his retreat, and on the hill where he was besieged after Benteen and McDougall joined him, numbered fifty-six dead and fifty-nine wounded, of whom eight died.

Of the six hundred who so confidently rode in review before Terry on the twenty-second, of the officers and men, veteran and recruit, of the proud Seventh Cavalry, there remained alive and fit for duty on the twenty-sixth, less than half; a loss of more than fifty-one per cent. In all history there is no such record of savage victory over trained troops.

What were the causes of the catastrophe? Who was to blame? Whose the responsibility? Controversy only slightly less savage and intense than that of the battle which gave it birth has raged for fifty years on these questions. And yet it is possible to answer them fairly without blasting the reputation of any participant or impugning the motives or the honesty of any military leader of that generation.

The chief cause of disaster was unquestion-

"Crow King": one of Gall's chief lieutenants.

ably and undeniably the lack of correct information as to the numbers, the organization, and the equipment of the Indians. The Seventh Cavalry was sent out by Terry to round up a band of recalcitrants variously estimated at between eight and fifteen hundred fighting men. They found almost three times the number of the highest estimate. They rode to locate and to drive or capture a band which, judged by all past experiences, would scatter and run at their approach; they found instead a force of stern warriors who fought with determination and tenacity equal to their own; who were led to battle by the greatest war-chiefs of the nation, whose strategy and tactical dispositions were that day superior to those of their opponents.

They thought to find a band equipped with ancient muskets and discarded rifles, with primitive spear and bow and arrow. Instead, they found a foe far better armed than they

[93]

themselves, possessing Winchester rifles of the latest pattern and stores of ammunition that seemed inexhaustible.

Why were these things not known? The answer lies in the almost criminal policy pursued by the Government during all the period of our Indian wars; a policy that permitted a maladministered Indian Bureau to sow the wind, and compelled the army to reap the whirlwind. It is idle now to discuss that policy: it has, happily, passed into history, a black, disgraceful page. But during the Indian war period the country resounded with its scandals and corruptions.

Next in importance as a causative factor was the failure of the expeditionary leaders to scout the country thoroughly; to obtain at first hand correct information of the enemy instead of relying upon the reports of Indian agents. Some effort was made, it is true, when Terry, some ten days before the battle, had sent Reno with half the Seventh Cavalry on the scouting expedition during which he had found the trail which Custer subsequently followed. But that effort was directed only to locating the hostiles. No real attempt appears to have been made to ascertain their strength before the movement against them was launched. (Note 17.)

Next in relative importance was the division of the regiment and the separation of its battalions beyond supporting distances. When Reno rode into the attack with his pitiful force of 112 men, his was the only part of the regiment on the western or village side of the river. His battalion, it is well to remember, was the only part of the regiment that at any time either crossed the Little Big Horn or was ordered to do so. Benteen's battalion was at this time miles away to the left and rear, its whereabouts unknown, and had no orders to coöperate either with Reno or with

Custer.   Reno, when he crossed the river, believed and had reason to believe that he was expected to bring on only an advance-guard action, and that Custer, with his larger and stronger force would deliver the main attack, supporting his charge from the rear.   But instead of supporting, Custer changed direction and rode five miles down the river without notifying Reno of his change of purpose, The pack-train, which with its escort accounted for 130 men, more than twenty per cent of the regiment, and which had in charge all the reserve of ammunition, had been left far back on the trail, to struggle along as best it might.   The men of the three battalions carried only one hundred rounds apiece of carbine ammunition, and four loadings, or twenty-four rounds, for their pistols.

When the fight in the valley began, therefore, not one of the three fighting battalions had ammunition sufficient for prolonged com-

"White-man-runs-him," one of Custer's Crow scouts who turned back in time to escape destruction.

bat, nor was within communicating distance of the reserve supply; nor was any one of the four detachments of the regiment within supporting distance of either of others. Not only were all separated by miles of difficult and enemy-infested country, but no one of the commanders, Custer, Reno, Benteen, or McDougall, knew where either of the others was, or what he was doing. This unfortunate separation, and, as it proved, fatal ignorance of each other's acts and whereabouts, gave to the Sioux, whose horde outnumbered the soldiers at least six to one, every opportunity to beat them in detail; opportunities of which they promptly and thoroughly availed themselves with almost Napoleonic sagacity.

It may be conjectured that Custer abandoned his expressed intention to support Reno's attack when he received word, through Cooke, that the Indians were coming up the valley in force to meet Reno's advance, for it was about that time, apparently, that he changed his course, left Reno's trail, and rode to the north. John Martin, the trumpeter who carried his message to Benteen to "come on and be quick," has stated that he heard the general say to his adjutant before the message was written that he would bring up Benteen and put him in the center while he attacked the rear. But this is the only scrap of evidence in existence as to what was in Custer's mind when he rode down the east bank of the river instead of following Reno to the other side.

Had the regiment been kept together and an attack delivered upon the village in the dashing, brilliant manner which had always characterized Custer's fighting, there was a chance to have driven or at least to have held the Sioux on even terms. But the Seventh Cavalry, even had it made the attempt as a unit, undivided, was too overwhelmingly outnumbered to have beaten them if they stood their ground or to have prevented their escape in any event.

Custer's defeat cannot fairly be ascribed to his disregard of Terry's plan of campaign. His disobedience of orders, if such occurred, and his disloyalty to his commander, if that existed, form no proper part of this narration. They constitute the basis for an inquiry of an entirely different nature. Both faults have been charged to Custer by his critics and his enemies; both have been indignantly denied by his supporters and his friends.

What would have happened had Terry's plan been followed to the letter is of course mere conjecture, but it is reasonably probable that if Custer, instead of following the trail of the Indians as he did, had scouted it only, and kept his force to the east, working south to the headwaters of the Tongue before turning toward the Little Big Horn, the Sioux would have discovered both his approach and Gibbon's, and the Indian village would have melted away and disappeared long before the jaws of Terry's trap could have closed upon them. And thus the whole purpose of the campaign must have failed.

One may surmise, of course, that the Sioux, having fought Crook to a standstill only the week before, might have held their position in the valley to await and receive just such an attack as Terry planned. They might, indeed, have advanced, to meet and crush Terry before Custer could come up; but the judgment of almost every Indian-fighter living is that they would not have done so. That they stood and fought as they did when the Seventh rode suddenly upon them on the twenty-fifth was in itself as surprising as it was unexpected; but it will not be forgotten that the Indians at the outset of the battle were fighting in defense of hearths and homes,

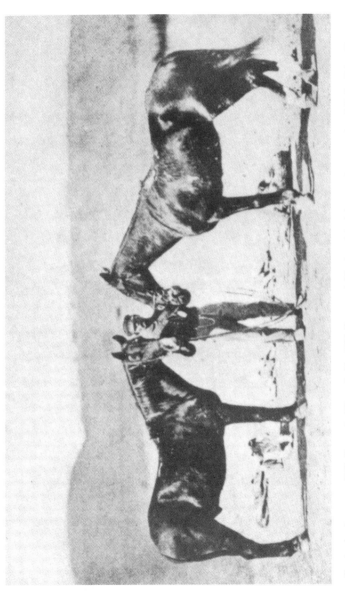

Custer's horses, "Vic" and "Dandy." "Vic" was killed with his master at the Little Big Horn. "Dandy," left with the pack train, came through unscathed, and was later sent to Custer's father at Monroe, Michigan.

and wives and children, and that the regiment's initial attack (Reno's) was pitifully weak. When Custer's approach was discovered, therefore, they knew well that every advantage, both of numbers and position, was theirs; that their own overwhelming force was between the widely separated bodies of white soldiers, one detachment of which they had just.driven in wild panic and utter rout.

What would have happened had Terry's plan been carried out is therefore speculation only. But the probable answer is: nothing; the Sioux would have separated and slipped away; there would have been no battle of the Little Big Horn; and Terry's expedition, like that of Crook and Reynolds before it, would have resulted in a mere water-haul.

VIII

SHORTLY after the battle, and long before the close of the campaign, there ensued much bitter comment and criticism over the conduct of Reno and Benteen, who were accused of disloyalty, disobedience of orders, and failure to go to Custer's relief. So strong and insistent did these claims become that Reno, finding himself discredited and all but ostracized, after vainly urging congressional investigation demanded a court of inquiry, which was held at Chicago during January, 1879, by order of the President. (Note 18.) The testimony developed during that extensive hearing failed to show that Reno had been remiss in his duty, but rather that he had been confronted with so overwhelming a force of Indians that to have charged into the village would inevitably have resulted in the total annihilation of his battalion. It indicated strongly that had he held his position in the timber, which he might have done for a somewhat longer period, the same result would probably have followed. Nor did it appear that his failure to charge the village or to hold the timber could in the least degree have affected Custer's fate. As to his alleged failure to go to the general's relief, it was abundantly proved that the thing was impossible even had Custer's extremity been known, which it was not; that Reno and Benteen combined could have effected nothing but their own slaughter had they advanced before arrival of the pack-train with ammunition. And this, unfortunately, came too late. Custer's fight was over.

The charges against Reno and Benteen took added strength from the known enmity of both men toward Custer; but it is as unthinkable as it is untrue that these officers deliberately sacrificed more than two hundred comrades, members of their own regiment, because of unfriendly feeling toward their commander: for that, in plain terms, was the charge against them in final analysis. There is nothing in the history of the fight on the Little Big Horn which justifies such a charge; it ought never to have been made, much less believed. On the contrary, while Reno did not show himself to be a great commander who could rise above the demands of trying and desperate conditions, it was due to his withdrawal from the valley, by whatever cause inspired (Note 19), and to Benteen's heroic leadership, that any of the Seventh Cavalry survived. The court of inquiry found nothing which required animadversion, and such was its unanimous report to the President. (Note 20.)

Sherman's telegram to Sheridan evidencing Grant's
displeasure with Custer.

It is highly significant that on July 4, 1876, only nine days after the battle, 236 of the enlisted men of the Seventh Cavalry, all of whom had participated in the action, joined in a petition to the President asking the promotion of Reno to the lieutenant-colonelcy of the regiment made vacant by Custer's death, and praying likewise for the advancement of Benteen to the grade of major. They did this in expression of their belief that these two officers had saved the regiment from utter annihilation. Had there existed in fact any such condition as the imputations against Reno and Benteen infer, it is beyond belief that such a request would have been almost unanimously made by the surviving enlisted men. (Note 21.)

Benteen was Custer's bitter and outspoken enemy. Not even death served to change his attitude; to the day of his own passing he never abated his hatred. But his known character and the habit of his entire life refutes the imputation that at any time or in any circumstances he failed in his duty as an officer and a soldier. He fought as he had lived, fearless, uncompromising, and grimly stern. Benteen was one of the best soldiers the United States Army has ever possessed.

For half a century the battle of the Little Big Horn has been known as the Custer Massacre. It is time that another name be given it, for it was no massacre. On the contrary it was a bitterly contested combat to the death between the armed representatives of two civilizations, each of which fought after the manner of his kind. The simple truth is that in this, the greatest battle ever waged between the red men and the white, between a receding and an advancing race, the red men had the victory because they exhibited that day a greater proficiency in the art of war than did the chosen representatives of the white men. Warfare, however it be savage, is not massacre when the conquered go to their deaths with arms in their hands.

In all Indian warfare mutilation of the bodies of the enemy dead as well as torture of living prisoners is expected. It is part and parcel of savage war. And therefore the battle of the Little Big Horn is all the more remarkable for the fact that there was no torture of prisoners, for the Sioux took none; and contrary to general belief there was no universal mutilation of the bodies of the slain, except those few of Reno's command who fell close to the village and were subjected to indignities by the squaws and children.

But on Custer's field, the Indian brave had in great part respected the bodies of his slain enemies. Save for scalping, the invariable custom of Indian warfare, there was compara-

[107]

tively little mutilation of the soldier dead. In a statement to the press; published just one month after the battle, Lieutenant Bradley, the scout chief of Terry who first saw and counted the dead, thus refuted the shocking tales of mutilation that had flooded the country:

Of the two hundred and six bodies buried on the field, there were very few that I did not see, and beyond scalping, in possibly a majority of cases, there was little mutilation. Many of the bodies were not even scalped, and in the comparatively few cases of disfiguration, it appeared to me the result rather of a blow with a knife, hatchet or war club to finish a wounded man than deliberate mutilation. . . . The bodies were nearly all stripped, but . . . I saw several entirely clothed, half a dozen at least. (Note 22.)

As for the body of the dead leader, it was found there white and undefiled. Perhaps there can be employed no better words to bring

The spot where Custer fell.

to a close this story of the Little Big Horn than Bradley's eloquent description of the dead Custer as he lay, like Saxon Harold at Hastings, surrounded by the bodies of his men-at-arms:

Probably never did hero who had fallen upon the field of battle appear so much to have died a natural death. His expression was rather that of a man who had fallen asleep and enjoyed peaceful dreams than of one who had met his death amid such fearful scenes as that field had witnessed, the features being wholly without ghastliness or any impress of fear, horror or despair. He had died as he lived, a hero.

NOTE 1

General Terry made two reports upon the battle of the Little Big Horn. The first, which was dated June 27, 1876, makes no mention of his plan of coöperative action by the columns of Custer and Gibbon. The second, which was intended to be confidential, was dated July 2, 1876. It reached Chicago in advance of the first report and while General Sheridan, to whom it was addressed, was in Philadalphia attending the Centennial Exposition. Sheridan, upon receipt of the confidential message, showed it to Sherman, then in command of the army, who was also in Philadelphia at the time. Sherman, desiring to relay the message to the Secretary of War at once, intrusted it to a person whom he supposed to be a Government messenger, but who proved to be a reporter for the "Philadelphia Inquirer." This enterprising journalist copied the message, and it appeared in full in the columns of the "Inquirer," July 7, 1876, and later, in the "Army and Navy Journal." It was the first official news of the disaster. The message follows:

I think I owe it to myself to put you more fully in possession of the facts of the late operations. While at the mouth of the Rosebud I submitted my plan to Genl. Gibbon and to General Custer. They approved it heartily. It was that Custer with his whole regiment should move up the Rosebud till he should meet a trail which Reno had discovered a few days before but that he should not follow it directly to the Little Big Horn; that he should send scouts over it and keep his main force further to the south so as to prevent the Indians from slipping in between himself and the mountains. He was also to examine the headwaters of Tullock's creek as he passed it and send me word of what he found there. A scout was furnished him for the purpose of crossing the country to me. We calculated it would take Gibbon's column until the twenty-sixth to reach the mouth of the Little Big Horn and that the wide sweep which I had proposed Custer should make would require so much time that Gibbon would be able to coöperate with him in attacking any Indians that might be found on that stream. I asked Custer how long his marches would be. He said they would be at first about thirty miles a day. Measurements were made and calculation based on that rate of progress. I talked with him about his strength and at one time suggested that perhaps it would be well for me to take Gibbon's cavalry and go with him. To this suggestion he replied that without reference to the command he would prefer his own regiment alone. As a homogeneous body, as much could be done with it as with the two combined and he expressed the utmost confidence that he had all the force that he could need, and I shared his confidence. The plan adopted was the only one that promised to bring the Infantry into action and I desired to make sure of things by getting up every available man. I offered Custer the battery of Gatling guns but he declined it saying that it might embarrass him: that he was strong enough without it. The movements proposed for Genl. Gibbon's column were carried out to the letter and had the attack been deferred until it was up I cannot doubt that we should have been successful. The Indians had evidently nerved themselves for a stand, but as I learn from Capt. Benteen, on the twenty-second the cavalry marched twelve miles; on the twenty-third, thirty-five miles; from five A. M till eight P. M. on the twenty-fourth, forty-five miles and then after night ten miles further; then after resting but without unsaddling, twenty-three miles to the battlefield. The proposed route was not taken but as soon as the trail was struck it was followed. I cannot learn that any examination of Tullock's creek was made. I do not tell you this to cast any reflection upon Custer. For whatever errors he may have committed he has paid the penalty and you cannot regret his loss more than I do, but I feel that our plan must have been successful had it been carried out, and I desire you to know the facts. In the action itself, so far as I can make out, Custer acted under a misapprehension. He thought, I am confident, that the Indians were running. For fear that they might get away he attacked without getting all his men up and divided his command so that they were beaten in detail. I do not at all propose to give the thing up here but I think that my troops require a little time and in view of the strength which the Indians have developed I propose to bring up what little reinforcement I can get. I should be glad of any that you can send me. I can take two companies of Infantry from Powder River and there are a few recruits and detached men whom I can get for the cavalry. I ought to have a larger mounted force than I now have but I fear cannot be obtained. I hear nothing from General Crook's operations. If I could hear I should be able to form plans for the future much more intelligently.

I should very much like instructions from you, or if not instructions, your views of the situation based as they might be on what has taken place elsewhere as well as here.

I shall refit as rapidly as possible and if at any time I should get information showing that I can act in conjunction with General Crook, or independently, with good results, I shall leave at once.

I send in another dispatch a copy of my written orders to Custer, but these were supplemented by the distinct understanding that Gibbon could not get to the Little Big Horn before the evening of the 26th.

ALFRED H. TERRY,
Brigadier General.

NOTE 2

General Terry's written instructions to Custer were as follows:

THE LITTLE BIG HORN

Lt. Col. Custer, 7th Cavalry:

Colonel:

The Brigadier General commanding directs that as soon as your regiment can be made ready for the march, you proceed up the Rosebud in pursuit of the Indians whose trail was discovered by Major Reno a few days ago. It is, of course, impossible to give you any definite instructions in regard to this movement, and were it not impossible to do so, the Department commander places too much confidence in your zeal, energy and ability to wish to impose upon you precise orders which might hamper your action when nearly in contact with the enemy.

He will, however, indicate to you his own views of what your action should be, and he desires that you should conform to them unless you shall see sufficient reason for departing from them. He thinks that you should proceed up the Rosebud until you ascertain definitely the direction in which the trail above spoken of leads. Should it be found, as it appears to be almost

certain that it will be found, to turn toward the Little
Big Horn he thinks that you should still proceed southward, perhaps as far as the headwaters of the Tongue,
and then turn toward the Little Big Horn, feeling constantly however, to your left so as to preclude the possibility of the escape of the Indians to the south or
southeast by passing around your left flank.

The column of Col. Gibbon is now in motion for the
mouth of the Big Horn. As soon as it reaches that
point it will cross the Yellowstone and move up at
least as far as the forks of the Big and Little Big Horn.
Of course its future movements must be controlled by
circumstances as they may arise; but it is hoped that
the Indians, if upon the Little Big Horn, may be so
nearly enclosed by the two columns that their escape
will be impossible.

The Department Commander desires that on your
way up the Rosebud you should thoroughly examine
the upper part of Tullocks Creek, and that you should
endeavor to send a scout through to Col. Gibbon's
column with information of the result of your exami-
naton. The lower part of this creek will be examined
by a detachment from Col. Gibbon's command.

The supply steamer will be pushed up the Big Horn as far as the forks of the river are found to be navigable for that space, and the Department Commander, who will accompany the column of Col. Gibbon, desires you to report to him there not later than the expiration of the time for which your troops are rationed, unless in the meantime you receive further orders.

Respectfully,

E. W. SMITH,

Capt. 18th Infantry,

Acting Asst. Adjt. Genl.

NOTE 3

The proportion of raw recruits in the Seventh Cavalry during the Little Big Horn campaign was very large. It has been impossible to ascertain the exact figures, for the rolls and returns of the regiment for 1876, which have been laboriously examined at Washington, do not contain the necessary data. Generals Edgerly and Godfrey, however, are authority for the statement that speaking in general terms, the companies contained from thirty to forty per cent of recruits without prior service. To very many of those, their first fight was their last.

During the proceedings of the Reno court of inquiry held at Chicago in 1879, Sergeant F. A. Culbertson, of Company A, testified (as to Reno's battalion) ;

Most of G Company were recruits; about half; and about a third of A Company. I don't know about M. The new men had had very little training; they were very poor horsemen and would fire at random. They were brave enough, but had not had the time nor opportunity to make soldiers. Some were not fit to take into action.

General Godfrey has lately informed the author that K Company took twenty-five recruits at St. Paul, just before the campaign opened. The total strength of the company after leaving the supply camp on the Yellowstone was forty-two, and these were disposed on June 25 as follows: with the pack-train, 7; with General Custer as flag-bearer, 1; hospital steward, 1; orderly to Dr. De Wolf, 1; total detached, 10. In action, 32, of whom 10 were detailed as horse-holders, leaving a fighting strength of 22.

NOTE 4

Statement of George Herendeen, scout, July 1, 1876, published in the "Army and Navy Journal," July 15, 1876:

About daylight we went into camp, made coffee, and soon after it was light, the scouts brought Custer word that they had seen the village from the top of a divide which separated the Rosebud from the Little Big Horn River. We moved up the creek until near its head and concealed ourselves in a ravine. It was about three miles from the head of the creek where we were then, to the top of the divide when the Indians scouts said the village could be seen. General Custer, with a few orderies, galloped forward to look at the Indian camp. In about an hour Custer returned and said he could not see the Indian village, but the scouts and a half-breed guide, "Mitch" Bouyer, said they could distinctly see it some fifteen miles off.

Testimony of Captain F. W. Benteen before the court of inquiry, 1879:

I think at the first halt (about 11:30 A. M., June 25), an orderly came to me with instructions for the officers to assemble. General Custer told us that he had just come down from the mountain; that he had been told by the scouts that they could see a village; ponies, tepees and smoke. He gave it to us as his belief that there were no Indians there; that he had looked through his glasses and could not see any and did not think there were any there.

Testimony of Major M. A. Reno before the court of inquiry, 1879:

At daylight I was informed only that the Commanding Officer had gone to the top of a mountain to make

"Rain-in-the-Face," the warrior who was said to have boasted that he killed Tom Custer and cut his heart out.

observation with regard to the Indians which the scouts had reported to be in sight. When he called the officers together, I attended, of course. He said the scouts had reported a large village in view from the mountain; that he did not believe it himself, as he had looked through his glass.

NOTE 5

Testimony of Captain Myles Moylan before the court of inquiry, 1879:

On the 25th at 10:30 to 11 o'clock, the command halted. There was a fresh trail visible, only a day or two old. While at this halt at the foot of the divide between the Little Big Horn and the Rosebud, a sergeant of one of the companies returned on the trail to recover some clothing of his that had been lost from a pack mule the night before. He had gone back several miles and while going over a knoll, saw two or three Indians four or five hundred yards in front of him, sitting on a box of hard bread and examining the contents of a bag. He returned at once and reported it to Capt. Yates, his company commander. Capt.

Yates talked it over with Capt. Keogh, and Keogh hunted up Colonel Cooke [the Adjutant] to notify him in order that General Custer might be informed. General Custer was at that time some distance ahead at the point where the Indian ponies were [reported to be] visible.

NOTE 6

It appears that information of the exodus of fighting men from the reservations reached Crook's command June 8, when despatches were received notifying him that all able-bodied male Indians had left the Red Cloud agency and that the Fifth Cavalry had been ordered up from Kansas to take post in his rear. See Bourke's "With Crook on the Border," pp. 295–296.

NOTE 7

It has been so often assumed that Custer, when he divided his regiment at the Little

Big Horn, had definitely planned to make an enveloping attack of the kind employed by him several years before at the Washita, that it is desirable to set out the reasons for the different view expressed in this narrative. These reasons are found in the testimony of his subordinate battalion commanders as given at the Reno inquiry at Chicago in 1879.

Benteen, who diverged to the left by Custer's order, at a few minutes after 12 M., testified:

When I received my orders from Custer to separate myself from the command, I had no instructions to unite with Reno or anyone else. There was no plan at all. . . .

If there had been any plan of battle, enough of that plan would have been communicated to me so that I would have known what to do under certain circumstances. Not having done that, I do not believe there was any plan. In General Custer's mind there was a belief that there were no Indians and no village. I do not know, except that I was sent off to hunt up some Indians. I was to pitch into them and let him know. And if I had found them, the distance would have been so great that we would have been wiped out before he could get to us.

Major Reno testified:

There was no plan communicated to us; if one existed, the subordinate commanders did not know of it. . . . When I say that no plan was communicated to us, I mean to the regiment. I do not think there was any plan.

That no definite plan of battle existed was evidently the belief of other officers. Lieutenant Wallace testified:

When we [first] crossed, Custer must have been to our right and rear; Benteen to our left and rear, but we knew nothing as to his orders and expected no assistance from him. I supposed from what Lieutenant Cooke said that our support would come from Custer, not Benteen. . . . There was no announcement made to Reno as to junction with Benteen that I know of. There was no plan for the reuniting of the three battalions that I ever heard of.

Sergeant Culbertson testified:

I heard Captain Weir ask Captain Moylan if, when he was Adjutant, General Custer ever gave him any particular orders about doing anything. Captain Moylan said "no," that when he was Adjutant, General Custer never told him what he was going to do: he would order him to tell company commanders to go to such and such places and that was all.

In an unpublished manuscript written by Benteen, found among his papers after his death, occurs the following:

. . . An orderly was sent to notify the officers that General Custer wished to see us: at all events the officers gathered where he was. General Custer then told us that he had just come down from the mountain where our Crow Indian scouts had been during the night, and that they had told him they could see tepee tops, lots of Indian ponies, dust, etc., but that he had looked through their telescopic glass, and that he could not see a thing, and he did not believe that they could see anything of the kind either.

This passage refers to the halt made by the regiment from 10:07 to 11:45 A. M. at the foot of the divide between the Rosebud and the Little Big Horn, when Custer went to the Crow's Nest to verify the report of the scouts. A few minutes afterward, the regiment crossed the divide, going about a mile, when the battalion division was made at 12:07 P. M., Benteen diverging to the left immediately thereafter.

NOTE 8

Testimony of Lieutenant George D. Wallace before the court of inquiry, 1879:

Lieutenant Cooke and Captain Keogh went with us toward the ford. Where they turned back I don't know.

NOTE 9

The situation of Reno's command immediately before he abandoned the position in the timber was graphically described by his officers during the inquiry at Chicago. Lieutenant Wallace of ˙G Company testified:

When we went on the skirmish line I for the first time saw the village, and the Indians were thick on our front and were pressing to our left and rear. After a short time it was reported that they were coming to the opposite bank and were trying to get our horses. Company G was taken off the line and put in the timber. The skirmish line soon had to fall back into the timber on account of exhaustion of ammunition and Indians on left and rear. After being there some time the Indians commenced firing from across the stream fifty yards from us and in our rear in the timber. There was no protection where we were, and the other side was a bank. Word was passed that we would have to charge them, as we were being surrounded. . . .

Lieutenant Varnum, in command of Reno's scouts said:

Captain Moylan called to me that the Indians were circling to the left and into the timber, and our horses and ammunition would be cut off and something must be done. . . . At the time the move was made a great many bullets were dropping into the woods from the rear. I did not see any Indians there, and whether the bullets came from the bluffs above or from below I don't know. The bottom near the stream was heavy with underbrush.

Captain Myles Moylan of A Company testified:

The horses were led into the timber for protection and the men deployed as skirmishers, G on the right, mine [A] in the center and M on the left. In about ten minutes I understood that Major Reno had information that the Indians were turning his right, coming up the left bank of the river, and the greater portion of G was withdrawn and taken into the woods, leaving an open space between the right of my company and the timber. I extended to cover that. . . .

I don't know how many Indians had got into the timber. I saw forty or fifty: there may have been several hundred. . . . The Indians in the timber next to the river were firing: 40 or 50 shots or more at the time we left.

Lieutenant De Rudio, in his testimony stated:

Lieutenant Wallace directed my attention to Indians coming in on the other side of the woods. I started over with five or six men to see. . . . I saw some Indians through the woods, downstream. . . . I noticed the company guidon on the bank . . . about 40 feet away. I crawled up and grabbed it. There were twenty or thirty Indians coming about 40 feet away. . . . They fired a volley at me. . . . There were about two hundred Indians on our right when we were in the timber.

George Herendeen, a civilian scout, testified:

The Indians come around our left and into the timber. As there was no firing on the line they came closer and closer. I saw twenty or twenty-five where I fired at them and more coming. . . . Major Reno was sitting on his horse in the park. I heard him order "dismount," and then there was a volley fired by the Indians. I judge the same ones I had seen coming in, and fired at. The Indians were not over thirty feet from us when they fired that volley.

NOTE 9½

Sgt. Heyn, erroneously reported killed in action, survived his serious wound, and lived to fight another day.

NOTE 10

General Godfrey has recently stated to the author that Lieutenant Gibson, in reply to his direct question, informed him that the last time he went to the top of the hills the valley of Little Big Horn was visible. This information was contained in a letter from Gibson to Godfrey dated August 8, 1908, in which

THE LITTLE BIG HORN

he says:

Now as to my little scout to the left to find the Little Big Horn valley, I can state definitely that I did find and see it. . . . Benteen sent me with a small detail . . . and he gave me his field glasses to take with me. I got some distance in advance . . . I crossed an insignificant stream running through a narrow valley which I knew was not the Little Big Horn, so I kept on to the high divide on the other side of it and from the top of it I could see plainly up the Little Big Horn valley for a long distance with the aid of the glasses; but in the direction of the village I could not see far on account of the sharp turns in it, or at any rate a turn which obstructed the view. I saw not a living thing in it and I hurried back and reported so to Benteen who then altered his course so as to pick up the trail, and you know the rest. I have often wondered what the result might have been if Benteen had taken his whole battalion to where he sent me, and then to have struck the village at some point other than where we did strke.

THE STORY OF
NOTE 11

Testimony of Captain F. W. Benteen before the court of inquiry, 1879:

From my orders I might have gone on twenty miles without finding a valley. Still I was to go on to the first valley and if I did not find any Indians I was to go on to the next valley. Those were the exact words of the order. . . . I understood it as a rather senseless order. . . . I consider that I violated my orders when I struck to the right. If I had carried them out I would have been twenty five miles away. . . . As it was, I was certainly too far to coöperate with Custer when he wanted me.

NOTE 12

See "Come On—Be Quick—Bring Packs," the complete story of Trumpeter Martin, "Cavalry Journal," July, 1923.

NOTE 13

It is a matter of great uncertainty as to the

time of the attack on Custer, with reference
to the time of Reno's retreat. Many of the
Indians have said that they did not fight Custer until after they whipped Reno. As to
those who were in the valley fight with Reno,
this is undoubtedly true. But the logic of the
whole situation, the time element, the distances traversed, and the fact that fully three
quarters of the Indian force was waiting for
Custer at the lower end of the village and am-
bushed him as soon as he turned toward the
river, impels the belief that the attack upon
him commenced some time before Reno's retreat. True, Reno's command heard the firing down river only after they arrived on the
hill; but that proves nothing, for while in action themselves, they would not have been
able to hear anything but the noise of their
own musketry. Lieutenant De Rudio, who
was left in the timber when the retreat was
made, testified before the court of inquiry in

1879:

Whether the Indians who left Reno to go down stream got there soon enough to assist in the attack on Custer I don't know. They started *after* the heavy firing commenced.

Reno was opposed largely by Hunkpapás and Blackfeet, who were camped at the upper or southern end of the village. The attack on Custer was begun by the Cheyennes and Ogalallas under Crazy Horse and Two Moon who were camped at the lower or northern end of the village. When Reno retreated, Gall, who had chased him to the river, dashed back to take charge of the attack on Custer from the south; and as soon as he arrived, he led the rush which crushed Calhoun and Keogh, while Crazy Horse and Two Moon were performing the same office as to the other companies of Custer's command.

Lieutenant Varnum testified before the court of inquiry:

[134]

THE LITTLE BIG HORN

The last time I saw Custer's command was about the time we dismounted in the bottom. I then saw the gray horse company moving down along the bluffs. I only saw it momentarily. It was back from the edge of the bluffs and the head and rear of the column were behind the edge of the bluffs. They were farther down stream than the point we struck in crossing, probably three quarters of a mile from where we then were in the bottom; they were moving at a trot. This was about an hour before Capt. Benteen joined us after we got on the hill. General Custer must have been in action before Benteen joined Reno.

NOTE 14

The following résumé of testimony given at the Reno inquiry clearly reflects the impressions and sentiments of the members of Reno's and Benteen's battalions regarding Custer's situation and whereabouts during the night of the twenty-fifth and shows beyond question that such a thing as his possible destruction never crossed their minds.

Lieutenant Wallace said:

After we occupied the hill there was no uneasiness about Custer; but there was a great deal of swearing about General Custer's running off and leaving us. . . . We were looking for him back the first night and didn't understand why we hadn't seen him. The command thought Custer had sent us in and then gone off and left us to look out for ourselves: that he had made an attack and probably been defeated, and had gone off down the river to meet General Terry.

Lieutenant (now General) Edgerly said:

Nobody had any idea that Custer was destroyed: the belief was general that he had gone to join Terry.

Lieutenant Varnum testified thus:

I suppose everybody felt as I did, wondering what had become of Custer and where he was. I don't know that there was any special worry—he had five companies with him. I don't think there was any idea or thought in the command that he was in the fix he was. The command felt in doubt, wondering if he was coralled as we were, or had been driven away to

Terry: but that he had been wiped out—there was no such thought. . . . When General Terry came up the first thing I asked was, "Where is Custer; do you know what has become of Custer?" and I supposed the cavalry of Terry's command was Custer.

And Lieutenant (now General) Godfrey stated:

There was an impression among the men that Custer had been repulsed and had abandoned them.

Benteen testified:

It was the belief of the officers on the hill during the night of the 25th that General Custer had gone off to join General Terry and that we were abandoned to our fate.

Captain McDougall of the rear-guard said:

During the night of the 25th the conclusion was that Custer had met the same crowd and they were either following him or else he had gone to join General Terry. . . . We had no idea that Custer's command was destroyed.

[137]

NOTE 15

Until the surrender of Kill Eagle, one of the older chiefs present at the battle, the contemporary press was filled with stories, probably sponsored by men of Reno's command, that the ranks of the Sioux contained many white allies. Indeed, Reno in his report said, "I think we were fighting all the Sioux Nation, and also all the desperadoes, renegades, half breeds and squaw men between the Missouri and the Arkansas and east of the Rocky Mountains."

One tale was that deserters from the army directed the Sioux attack; another that a cashiered West-Pointer had drilled the warriors and instructed them in tactics. Still another, that they had learned the army's bugle signals and employed a deserter trumpeter to blow the war chief's orders on his bugle.

All these stories proved figments of imagination, and when Kill Eagle gave himself up he put them all at rest. No whites fought in the Indian ranks, and the bugle-calls were blown by a warrior upon a captured trumpet!

NOTE 15½

No authentic information as to the Indian loss at the Little Big Horn has ever been available. After the hurried departure of the Sioux, two tepees containing the dead bodies of some twenty-two warriors were found standing in the village. The bodies were dressed as for burial, and the tepees were surrounded by the bodies of ponies, arranged in accord with savage burial custom. Several more bodies were discovered along the trail taken by the Indians, these being sepultured in trees and on scaffolds.

Altogether, about forty dead were thus accounted for; some of these, however, were probably casualties of Crook's fight on the

Rosebud, which occurred on June 17. How many of the Indians were wounded at the Little Big Horn, or died of wounds received in the battle, no one has ever known.

NOTE 16

According to General Godfrey's talley, which is undoubtedly correct, 212 bodies were recovered. Lieutenant Bradley in his letter of July 25, 1876 (see Note 22), gives the number as 206. Godfrey's, however, included the bodies found in the village.

The exact number of men with Custer is not known. It was, however, about 225. The bodies of several, both officers and men, were never found, or, if found, never identified. They had lain in the hot sun three days when burial took place, and the difficulty of identification in many cases is not to be wondered at.

The battle of the Little Big Horn was hardly over when alleged witnesses or survivors began to appear. Even now, fifty years after the event, it is no infrequent occurrence to find some enterprising imagination still at work, whose owner comes forward with spurious claims. There is no truth in any of these tales. No authentic witnesses save the Sioux have ever appeared, and their accounts are at such variance that it is impossible to reconcile them. It was long believed that Curley, a Crow scout, went into the fight with Custer and escaped in disguise; but his story has been completely discredited by the other Crow scouts who were his companions that day.

NOTE 17

Reno, on returning from his scout, reported that the trail he struck on the Rosebud was of a band of some three hundred lodges. This appears to have been the only late information the regiment possessed as to the enemy's strength.

NOTE 18

The immediate cause of Reno's demand for a court of inquiry was a letter addressed by Custer's biographer, Frederick Whittaker, to the Hon. W. W. Corlett, a delegate to Congress from Wyoming, in which he vitriolically urged a congressional investigation of the conduct of both Reno and Benteen, against whom he made the most serious of charges. The letter was dated May 18, 1878, and Reno's demand for a court of inquiry followed its publication on June 13, 1878, his letter to the President being dated June 22, 1878. He had previously urged the Military Committee of the House to resolve upon the inquiry asked by Whittaker, but Congress had adjourned without action. Reno's critics have always insisted that he made no move to clear his record until the statute of limitations had barred trial by court martial. While it is true that he did not demand a court of inquiry as promptly as another might have done, it is equally true that during all the time intervening between the battle and his demand for such a court, no charges were ever preferred against him.

NOTE 19

Whether Major Reno was justified in leaving the timber, whether his movement to the hills was inspired by cowardice, whether his conduct throughout the action was craven, are questions about which there will be dispute and controversy so long as the battle of the Little Big Horn is remembered. This narrative is not intended as support to either side; it simply endeavors to state "the haps as they happened." Reno's conduct of the action in the valley has been so bitterly assailed, however, and he has been so unsparingly condemned by authors who have written of the

Little Big Horn fight, both for his failure to charge into the village and for his retreat to the hills, that it is only fair to him that the opinions of the officers and men who were with him, as they gave them under oath during the inquiry at Chicago in 1879, he made known.

The following extracts give these opinions as they were expressed upon the witness-stand by every surviving officer of his battalion except Captain French of M Company, who was not called, and by the only enlisted man whose opinion was asked:

FAILURE TO CHARGE INTO THE VILLAGE

Lieutenant Luther R. Hare, Scouts:

If Reno had continued to advance mounted, I don't think he would have got a man through: the column would not have lasted five minutes. His dismounting and deploying was all that saved us.

THE LITTLE BIG HORN

Captain Myles Moylan, A Company:

In my judgment if he [Reno] had continued to
charge down the valley he would have been there yet.
In my judgment the command, without assistance,
would have been annihilated in the timber. If the
Indians had followed and closed in on the retreat to
the bluffs the same result would have followed.

Lieutenant Charles De Rudio, A Company:

I saw no indications of cowardice on Reno's part;
nor any want of skill in the handling and disposition
of men. When he halted and dismounted I said,
"Good for you," because I saw that if we had gone
500 yards further we would have been butchered.

RETIREMENT OF THE SKIRMISH-LINE

Sergeant Culbertson, G Company:

If the skirmish line had not been retired, or had been
held out there three minutes longer, I don't think any
one would have gotten off the line. I don't think

Major Reno could have held the timber but a very few minutes.

LEAVING THE TIMBER IN RETREAT

Lieutenant George D. Wallace, G Company:

I think Reno did the only thing possible under the circumstances. If we had remained in the timber all would have been killed. It was his duty to take care of his command and to use his best judgment and discretion.

Lieutenant Charles A. Varnum, Scouts:

The position in the timber was as good as any place on the left bank. But I don't think we had enough men to hold it and keep the Indians out of it. The front was good; but I don't know about the rear. At the time the move was made a great many bullets were dropping into the woods from the rear.

Lieutenant L. R. Hare, Scouts:

Major Reno stayed in the timber till all hope of support from Custer had vanished. I think the reason we left was because if we stayed much longer, say twenty minutes, we could not have gotten out at all. . . . I can only estimate his conduct by the way it turned out. I think his action saved what was left of the regiment.

KNOWLEDGE OF EXPECTATION OF REINFORCEMENT BY BENTEEN

Major M. A. Reno:

At the time I left the timber I did not see Benteen's column nor had I the remotest reason to expect him to unite with me.

Captain F. W. Benteen:

When I received my orders from Custer to separate myself from the command I had no instructions to unite at any time with Reno or anyone else. There was no plan at all. . . . The reason I returned was because I thought I would be needed at the ridge. I acted entirely upon my own judgment. I was separated from Reno fifteen miles when at the greatest distance. . . . My going back was providential or accidental or whatever you may be pleased to term it.

General Winfield Scott Edgerly, who was Weir's lieutenant during the battle, and whose knowledge and information equals that of any officer of Benteen's battalion, does not consider that Reno was cowardly. On the contrary, he says in a recent letter to the author that while, in common with all his command, Reno was intensely excited when he reached the hills, he soon calmed down, and thereafter "was perfectly cool, though by no means heroic."

On the other hand, General Edward S. Godfrey, who commanded K Company, of Benteen's battalion, during the action on the hill, thinks that Reno was cowardly and craven throughout. When called as a witness at Chicago, however, he did not plainly state that opinion, but characterized what he himself observed as "nervous timidity."

The late General Nelson A. Miles condemned Reno in the strongest of terms, as does also another very distinguished veteran of the Indian wars, Captain R. G. Carter (retired), late of the Fourth Cavalry, Mackenzie's regiment. As neither General Miles nor Captain Carter was present at the Little Big Horn, their opinions are necessarily based upon hearsay and report.

Edgerly, Godfrey, Varnum, and Hare are the only officers of the Seventh of 1876 who now survive. The opinions of both Varnum and Hare, who of the four were the only ones who participated in the valley fight, have already been quoted verbatim, just as they gave them from the witness-stand in 1879.

From the foregoing résumé, it appears that in the opinion of his own officers Reno exercised proper discretion and good leadership up to the time his retreat to the hills began, and that the dispositions and movements ordered by him were correct and requisite to meet the military situation. From that time on, however, it seems evident that he lost his head, and, with it, all control over his men. When Bloody Knife was killed at his side, he became startled and unnerved. His formations were made in undue haste, and many men were left behind who neither heard nor understood the order to leave the timber. The run to the river became a panic, and when those who successfully ran the gauntlet reached the bluffs, they were halted with difficulty. Reno at no time thereafter regained his lost leadership, and it was Benteen whose "providential" arrival saved the day and what was left of the regiment.

FIRE-CONTROL

There appears to have been little or no fire-control during the fight in the valley. The men shot away their ammunition both reck-lessly and rapidly, and when the survivors reached the hills, more than half their scanty store had been expended. For this, Reno has been bitterly assailed, and not with entire justice.

There is no doubt that with seasoned troops proper fire-control is always *possible*. It is by no means always had, however. *But with ranks full of raw recruits, the difficulty of fire-control immeasurably increases.*

Reno's seasoned men were necessarily de-tailed as horse-holders, and thus his firing-line was filled with men who never before had been in action. Complete fire-control is impossible under such conditions, however great its need; and it is in every situation the responsibility, primarily, of the platoon and company commanders. While Reno, as battalion com-mander, is properly subject to a share of criti-cism, it is they, rather than he, who should bear the greater burden of blame for its apparent total absence during the fight in the valley.

NOTE 20

The court of inquiry convened at Major Reno's request sat at Chicago during January, 1879. Colonel John H. King, Ninth Infantry, was president. Colonel Wesley Merritt, Fifth Cavalry, and Colonel William B. Royall, Third Cavalry, completed the membership. After a long and protracted hearing, during which some twenty-three witnesses were examined, the court came to its findings, which were thereafter published by the War Department, as follows:

General Orders ⎱ HEADQUARTERS OF THE ARMY,
No. 17. ⎰   Adjutant General's Office,
                  Washington, March 11 1879.

1. The Court of Inquiry of which Colonel John H. King, 9th Infantry, is President, instituted by direc-

From a photo by Copelin.

A newspaper cut of the Reno Court of Inquiry held at Chicago in 1879.

tion of the President, in Special Orders No. 255, Headquarters of the Army, Adjutant General's Office, November 25, 1878, on the application of Major Marcus A. Reno, 7th Cavalry, for the purpose of inquiring into Major Reno's conduct at the battle of the Little Big Horn River, on the 25th ond 26th days of June, 1876, has reported the following facts and opinions, viz:—

First. On the morning of the 25th of June 1876, the 7th Cavalry, Lieutenant Colonel G. A. Custer commanding, operating against the hostile Indians in Montana Territory, near the Little Big Horn River, was divided into four battalions, two of which were commanded by Colonel Custer in person, with the exception of one company in charge of the pack-train; one by Major Reno and one by Captain Benteen. This division took place from about twelve (12) to fifteen (15) miles from the scene of the battle or battles afterwards fought. The column under Captain Benteen received orders to move to the left for an indefinite distance (to the first and second valleys) hunting Indians, with orders to charge any it might meet with. The battalion under Major Reno received orders to draw out of the column, and doing so marched parallel [with] and only a short distance from, the column commanded by Colonel Custer.

Second. About three or four miles from what afterwards was found to be the Little Big Horn River, where the fighting took place, Major Reno received orders to move forward as rapidly as he thought prudent, until coming up with the Indians, who were reported fleeing, he would charge them and drive everything before him, and would receive the support of the column under Colonel Custer.

Third. In obedience to the orders given by Colonel Custer, Captain Benteen marched to the left (south), at an angle of about forty-five degrees, but, meeting an impracticable country, was forced by it to march more to his right than the angle above indicated and nearer approaching a parallel route to that trail followed by the rest of the command.

Fourth. Major Reno, in obedience to the orders given him, moved on at a fast trot on the main Indian trail until reaching the Little Big Horn River, which he forded, and halted for a few minutes to re-form his battalion. After re-forming, he marched the battalion forward towards the Indian village, down stream or in a northerly direction, two companies in line of battle and one in support, until about half way to the point where he finally halted, when he brought the company in reserve forward to the line of battle, continuing the movement at a fast trot or gallop until after passing over a distance of about two miles, when he halted and dismounted to fight on foot at a point of timber upon which the right flank of his battalion rested. After fighting in this formation for less than half an hour, the Indians passing to his left rear and appearing in his front, the skirmish line was withdrawn to the timber, and the fight continued for a short time—half an hour or forty-five minutes in all—when the command, or nearly all of it, was mounted, formed, and, at a rapid gait, was withdrawn to a hill on the opposite side of the river. In this movement one officer and about sixteen soldiers and citizens were left in the woods, besides one wounded man or more, two citizens and thirteen soldiers rejoining the command afterwards. In this retreat Major Reno's battalion lost some twenty-nine men in killed and wounded, and three officers, including Doctor De Wolf, killed.

Fifth. In the meantime Captain Benteen, having carried out, as far as was practicable, the spirit of his orders, turned in the direction of the route taken by the remainder of the regiment, and reaching the trail, followed it to near the crossing of the Little Big Horn, reaching there about the same time Reno's command was crossing the river in retreat lower down, and finally joined his battalion with that of Reno, on the hill. Forty minutes or one hour later the pack-train, which had been left behind on the trail by the rapid movement of the command and the delays incident to its march, joined the united command, which then consisted of seven companies, together with about thirty (30) or thirty-five (35) men belonging to the companies under Colonel Custer.

Sixth. After detaching Benteen's columns Colonel Custer moved with his immediate command, on the trail followed by Reno, to a point within about one mile of the river, where he diverged to the right (or northward), following the general direction of the river to a point about four miles below that (afterward taken by Major Reno) where he and his command were destroyed by the hostiles. The last living witness of this march, Trumpeter Martin, left Colonel Custer's command when it was about two miles distant from the field where it afterwards met its fate. There is nothing more in evidence as to this command, save that firing was heard proceeding from its direction from about the time Reno retreated from the bottom up to the time the pack-train was approaching the position on the hill. All firing which indicated fighting was concluded before the final preparations [were made] in Major Reno's command for the movement which was afterwards attempted.

Seventh. After the distribution of ammunition and a proper provision for the wounded men, Major Reno's entire command moved down the river in the direction it was thought Custer's column had taken, and in which it was known General Terry's command was to be found. This movement was carried sufficiently far to discover that its continuance would imperil the entire command, upon which it returned to the position formerly occupied, and made a successful resistance till succor reached it. The defense of the position on the hill was a heroic one against fearful odds.

The conduct of the officers throughout was excellent,

and while subordinates, in some instances, did more for the safety of the command by brilliant displays of courage than did Major Reno, there was nothing in his conduct which requires animadversion from this Court.

Opinion

It is the conclusion of this Court, in view of all the facts in evidence, that no further proceedings are necessary in this case, and it expresses this opinion in compliance with the concluding clause of the order convening the Court.

II. The proceedings and opinion of the Court of Inquiry in the foregoing case of Major Marcus A. Reno, 7th Cavalry, are approved by order of the President.

III. By direction of the Secretary of War, the Court of Inquiry of which Colonel John H. King, 9th Infantry, is President is hereby dissolved.

By command of General Sherman:

E. D. Townsend,
Adjutant General.

Official.

The petition of the surviving enlisted men of the regiment asking the promotions of Reno and Benteen.

(Continued on Following Page)

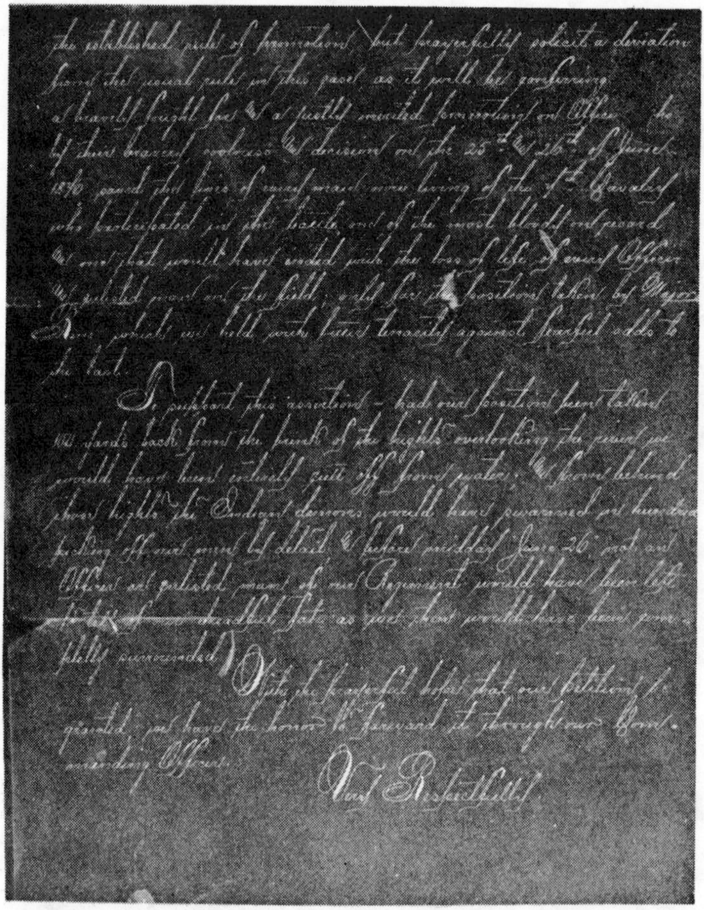

(Continued From Preceding Page)

NOTE 21

Camp near Big Horn on Yellowstone River,

July 4th, 1876.

To his

Excellency the President

and the Honorable Representatives

of the United States.

Gentlemen:

We the enlisted men the survivors of the battle on the Heights of Little Horn River, on the 25th and 26th of June 1876, of the 7th Regiment of Cavalry who subscribe our names to this petition, most earnestly solicit the President and Representatives of our Country, that the vacancies among the Commissioned Officers of our Regiment, made by the slaughter of our brave, heroic, now lamented Lieutenant Colonel George A. Custer, and the other noble dead Commissioned Officers of our Regiment who fell close by him on the bloody field, daring the savage demons to the last, be filled by the Officers of the Regiment only. That Major M. A. Reno, be our Lieutenant Colonel vice Custer, killed; Captain F. W. Benteen our Major vice Reno, promoted. The other vacancies to be filled by officers of the Regiment by seniority. Your petitioners know this to be contrary to the established rule of promotion, but prayerfully solicit a deviation from the usual rule in this case, as it will be conferring a bravely fought for and a justly merited promotion on officers who by their bravery, coolness and decision on the 25th and 26th of June 1876, saved the lives of every man now living of the 7th Cavalry who participated in the battle, one of the most bloody on record and one that would have ended with the loss of life of every officer and enlisted man on the field only for the position taken by Major Reno, which we held with bitter tenacity against fearful odds to the last.

To support this assertion—had our position been taken 100 yards back from the brink of the heights overlooking the river we would have been entirely cut off from water; and from behind those heights the Indian demons would have swarmed in hundreds picking off our men by detail, and before midday June 26th not an officer or enlisted man of our Regiment would have been left to tell of our dreadful fate as we then would have been completely surrounded.

With prayerful hope that our petitions be granted, we have the honor to forward it through our Commanding Officer.

Very Respectfully,
[236 signatures]

This petition went to General Sherman, who did not present it to the President or to Congress, but indorsed it as follows:

Headquarters Army of the United States, Washington, D. C., August 5, 1876.

The judicious and skilful conduct of Major Reno and Captain Benteen is appreciated, but the promotions caused by General Custer's death have been made by the President and confirmed by the Senate; therefore this petition cannot be granted. When the Sioux campaign is over I shall be most happy to recognize the valuable services of both officers and men by granting favors or recommending actual promotion.

Promotion on the field of battle was Napoleon's favorite method of stimulating his officers and soldiers to deeds of heroism, but it is impossible in our service because commissions can only be granted by the President on the advice and consent of the Senate, and except in original vacancies, promotion in a regiment is generally if not always made on the rule of seniority.

W. T. SHERMAN,
General.

NOTE 22

The letter of Lieutenant Bradley (quoted in the text) in which he recounts the circumstances under which he discovered the Custer battle-field on the morning of June 27, 1876, and describes the condition of the bodies of the soldier dead, was published in the Helena (Montana) "Herald" for July 25, 1876. It is as follows:

Reports current in the States, circulated by many papers, of the mutilation of Custer's body, are disposed of by Lt. Bradley in a letter published in our columns

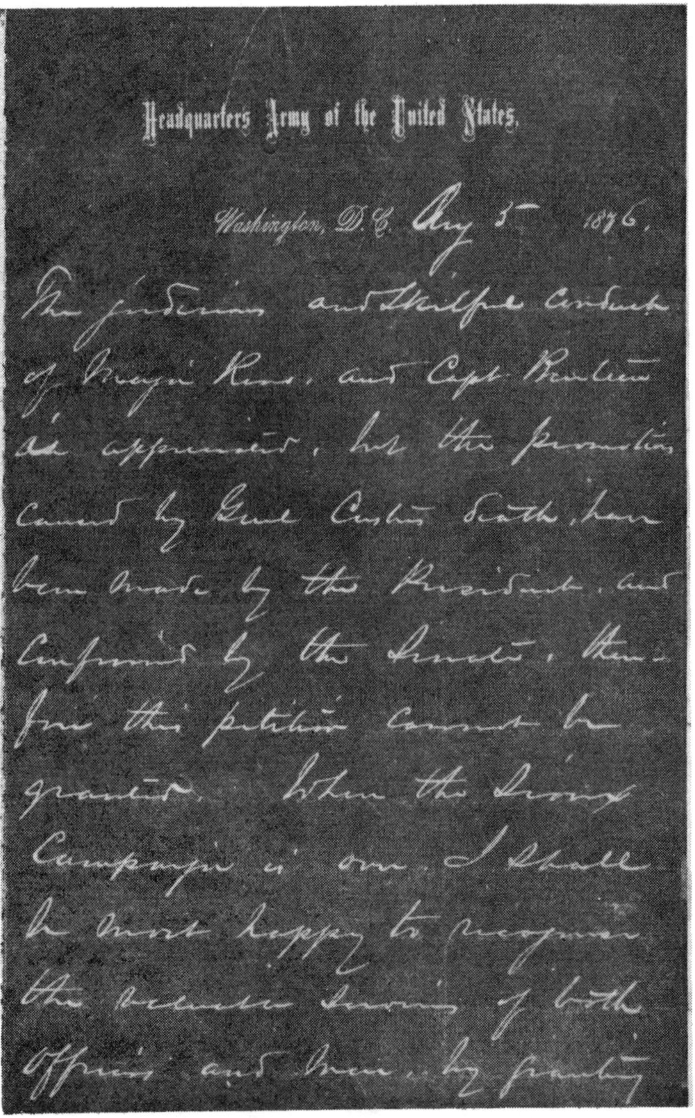
Headquarters Army of the United States,

Washington, D.C. Aug 5th 1876.

The gallantry and skillful conduct of Major Reno, and Capt Benteen is appreciated, but the promotions caused by Genl Custer's death, have been made by the President and confirmed by the Senate, therefore this petition cannot be granted. When the Sioux Campaign is over I shall be most happy to recognize the valuable services of both officers and men, by granting

General Sherman's action on the enlisted men's petition.

(Continued on Following Page)

from . . . recommending actual promotion. Promotion on the Field of Battle was . . . favorite method of stimulating his officers and soldiers to deeds of heroism, but it . . . is impossible in our service because Commissions can only be granted by the President on the advice and consent of the Senate, and except in original vacancies, promotion in a Regiment is generally if not always made on the rule of seniority.

W. T. Sherman
General.

(Continued From Preceding Page)

today. It is not true that Custer's heart was cut out by the savages, or that his remains otherwise suffered disfigurement.

"Helena, M. T.

"July 25, 1876.

"To the Editor of the Herald,

"In the presence of so great a disaster as that which overtook the regular troops on the Little Horn, and the consequent excited state of the public mind, and its eagerness to get hold of every detail, however minute, of that unfortunate affair, it is to be expected that many stories of a sensational character, having no foundation in truth, would obtain with the public. Of such character is that now going the rounds of the press to the effect that the Sioux had removed Custer's heart from his body and danced around it, a story related upon the authority of one Rain-in-the-Face, a Sioux Chief, who participated in the fight and afterwards returned to his agency. Of the same character, also, is the sweeping statement as to the general shocking mutilation of the bodies of the soldiers who fell on that occasion. The bare truth is painful enough to the relatives and friends of these unfortunate men

[163]

without the cruel and gratuitous exaggeration of their grief that must come from the belief that they had been horribly mutilated after death. It, therefore, seems to me worth while that these stories should receive emphatic contradiction, and being in a position to make such a denial, I address you this letter with that object.

"In my capacity as commandant of the Scouts accompanying General Gibbon's column, I was usually in the advance in all his movements, and chanced to be upon the morning ·of the 27th of June, when the column was moving upon the supposed Indian village in the Little Horn Valley. I was scouting the hills some two or three miles to the left of the column upon the opposite bank of the river from that traversed by the column itself, when the body of a horse attracted our attention to the field of Custer's fight, and hastening in that direction the appalling sight was revealed to us of his entire command in the embrace of death. This was the first discovery of the field, and the first hasty count made of the slain, resulting in the finding of 197 bodies reported to General Terry. Later in the day I was sent to guide Colonel Benteen of the 7th

Cavalry to the field, and was a witness of his recognition of the remains of Custer. Two other officers of that regiment were also present and they could not be mistaken, and the body so identified was wholly unmutilated. Even the wounds that caused his death were scarcely discoverable (though the body was entirely naked), so much so that when I afterwards asked the gentlemen whom I accompanied whether they had observed his wounds, they were forced to say that they had not.

"Probably never did hero who had fallen upon the field of battle appear so much to have died a natural death. His expression was rather that of a man who had fallen asleep and enjoyed peaceful dreams, than of one who had met his death amid such fearful scenes as that field had witnessed, the features being wholly without ghastliness or any impress of fear, horror or despair. He had died as he lived, a hero, and excited the remark from those who had known him and saw him there, 'You could almost imagine him standing before you.' Such was Custer at the time of his burial on the 28th of June, three days after the fight in which he had fallen, and I hope this assurance will

dispose of the horrible tale of the mutilation and dese-
cration of his remains.

"Of the 206 bodies buried on the field, there were
very few that I did not see, and beyond scalping, in
possibly a majority of cases, there was little mutilation. Many of the bodies were not even scalped, and
in the comparatively few cases of disfiguration, it appeared to me the result rather of a blow with a knife,
hatchet, or war club to finish a wounded man, than deliberate mutilation. Many of Custer's men must have
been disabled with wounds during the fight, and when
the savages gained possession of the field, such would
probably be mainly killed in the manner indicated.
The bodies were nearly all stripped, but it is an error
to say that Kellogg, the correspondent, was the only
one that escaped this treatment. I saw several entirely clothed, half a dozen at least, who, with Kellogg,
appeared to owe this immunity to the fact that they
had fallen some distance from the field of battle, so
that the Indians had not cared to go to them, or had
overlooked them when the plundering took place.

"The real mutilation occurred in the case of Reno's

men, who had fallen near the village. These had been visited by the squaws and children and in some instances the bodies were frightfully butchered. Fortunately not many were exposed to such a fate. Custer's field was some distance from the village and appears not to have been visited by these hags, which probably explains the exemption from mutilation of those who had fallen there.

"Yours truly,

"JAMES H. BRADLEY,

"1st Lieut. 7th Inft."

It is proper to state for the reader's information that such authorities as James McLaughlin, author of "My Friend the Indian," who for many years was Indian agent at Standing Rock, does not accept Lieutenant Bradley's statement as correct; on the contrary, he states in the work referred to that the mutilation of bodies on the Custer field was both general and shocking. Mr. Amos Gottschall of Harrisburg, Pennsylvania, another man who had long experience among the Indians, echoes McLaughlin's views. On the other hand, W. M. Camp of Chicago, who for twenty years spent his summers among the plains tribes, says that Custer's conquerors, hundreds of whom he interviewed, very generally support what Bradley said as true.

CONCLUDING NOTE

Few white men, even in the "old days," were ever able to understand the Indian's point of view, and fewer still were able to comprehend his motives. His psychology was a field almost untouched. The Indian lived in a different world to ours, and his ideas and traditions, his customs, his beliefs and superstitions were as different from those of the white man as the poles are far apart. As well attempt to measure the ancient Phenician by the standards of the primal Briton, or to judge the Zulu warrior by comparing him with the Chinese.

The story of an Indian campaign, to be comprehensible to white men, must be written from the white man's point of view, and this narrative is written from that point of view. There have been, perhaps, exceptional white men who from long and friendly intercourse and sympathetic contact have learned the psychology of the Indian; but those living to-day who thus knew the plains Indian of a half-century ago, when his race was strong and powerful, before he had succumbed to the domination of the white man, are so few that they may easily be counted. They were never numerous, and the author makes no claim to membership among them.

Therefore no attempt has been made to set forth the Indian viewpoint, or to include any of the various accounts of the battle related by individual Indians, for the result would almost inevitably have been misconstruction and distortion. The Indian accounts vary so widely upon nearly every salient fact as to seem irreconcilable to the white man's logic. They are sparse and hard to understand. They do not check with one another. Therefore, no effort has been made to use them.

It is, however, not difficult to account for the paucity and lack of agreement in the tales told by the Indians. After the battle, notwithstanding their overwhelming victory, the tribes separated and scattered to the four winds. Some of them soon returned to the reservations, as did Kill Eagle and his followers; others remained out until forced back by the vicissitudes to which they were subject, as did Crazy Horse and his band. Pursued everywhere by relentless troops, many were killed; others were captured or surrendered. Sitting Bull with his own band escaped to Canada, where he remained for several years.

When the "hostiles" came in, they came as suppliants or as conquered, if not as captives. They both feared and expected punishment for the part they had taken in the wiping out of Custer's command. *Væ victis* was the only rule they knew. It was natural that they should tell as little as they might; and notwithstanding promised amnesty, they did not believe the white man would keep faith. Each warrior's tale was therefore his individual story, too often shaped to please the ear of his white interrogator.

The tribal organizations were disrupted, the chiefs supplanted by new and strange leaders who had not the authority or the influence of the old ones; the power of the councils was gone. No more did their own form of government prevail, but that of the white man. The Indian's world was upside down, his freedom gone.

"No more did the teller of tales wander

among the tepees, feasting upon the choicest morsels of the tent dweller's fare, while reciting to rapt audiences the legends and folk lore of his people; no more did the criers stalk through the camps, intoning the orders of the council, summoning the people to ceremonial dances; to tribal hunts and solemn rites."

And so no Indian saga of this greatest of their triumphs over the paleface; no Siouan epic of the red avalanche that overbore the Yellow Hair and his cohorts was ever sung. Nor will it be. The day of the red man has passed forever; the stronger hand of another, and to him a stifling, civilization has slowly but surely choked him until his racial soul is dead.

The author has endeavored in the foregoing pages and notes to present a vivid and faithful picture of the great contest between the Sioux and the troops of Custer. The narrative is not offered as a complete history of the campaign of 1876, nor does it pretend to relate in detail all that occurred on that fateful twenty-fifth of June. To compass either would require a volume of considerable size. But it is believed that the important and salient facts will be found here, and that from this story the uninitiated reader may be enabled to visualize the battle as it occurred.

It should be understood that from the time of the division of the Seventh Cavalry into battalions just after crossing the divide between the Rosebud and the Little Big Horn valleys, about noon of June 25, all time periods as well as distances are necessarily approximated. These have been carefully computed after analysis of all the authentic data discoverable after a study and search extending over several years. They are believed to be nearly correct and, in the main, to approach the truth as closely as it is now possible to do. The map which appears at page

29 is believed to show more accurately the movements of the Seventh Cavalry on the day of the battle than any heretofore published.

W. A. GRAHAM,
Colonel, Judge Advocate,
U. S. Army, Retired.
Pacific Palisades, California
May, 1941.

APPENDIX I

DID CUSTER WILFULLY DISOBEY HIS ORDERS?

For years the author has been importuned by students, critics and historians alike, to discuss the highly controversial question whether Custer wilfully disobeyed Terry's orders. He has consistently declined to do so. To satisfy such demands, however, there is here reproduced in the following appendix, the most complete and extended discussion of that subject of which he has any knowledge. Its author, the late General R. P. Hughes, was Terry's Aide and Chief of Staff during the Sioux War of 1876, and his article, published in January 1896, as a reply to General Fry's comments on General (then Captain) Godfrey's narative of the campaign (Century, 1892), attracted wide attention, and induced an interesting and informative debate, participated in by Generals Hughes, Godfrey, Miles, Carrington, Woodruff, and Forsyth, which should also be read by every student of the campaign. It appeared as an appendix to Cyrus Townsend Brady's "Indian Fights and Fighters" at pages 359-397. The debate centered about the validity of an affidavit supposed to be in General Miles possession, allegedly made by "the last witness who heard the two officers (Terry and Custer) in conversation together", and quoted Terry as having said: "Use your own judgment, and do what you think best if you strike the trail;***". Since Dr. Brady's book was published, however, the identity of the affidavit maker, then known only to General Miles, has been established as one Mary Adams, a colored woman at one time employed by Custer as a cook. The affidavit is worthless, as both Generals Godfrey and Edgerly, and Colonel Varnum also, assured the author during 1924 that its maker, Mary Adams, neither accompanied the troops nor was present at any time during the campaign. During the same year, the author interviewed General Miles concerning this affidavit, but gained no information as to how it was obtained. All General Miles would say about it was— "I believe Mrs. Custer has it". The Notary before whom the affidavit was taken, though located, was unable to recall the circumstances.

The Journal of the Military Service Institution of the United States, in which the Hughes article appeared, long since passed out of existence, and the article, never reprinted, is unobtainable and to be found only in exceptional military libraries. It is appended here without comment, except by way of caution. Readers should remember that to every controversial question there are two sides, and that between wilful disobedience of orders and justifiable disregard of instructions there yawns a gulf both wide and deep.

That Custer did disregard Terry's instructions seems reasonably clear: whether he was justified in doing so is a question that will bear examination. The Commander on the scene is entitled to the benefit of every doubt, if there be room for doubt; and particularly is this true when neither he, nor any other who may have known his reasons, survived to present them.

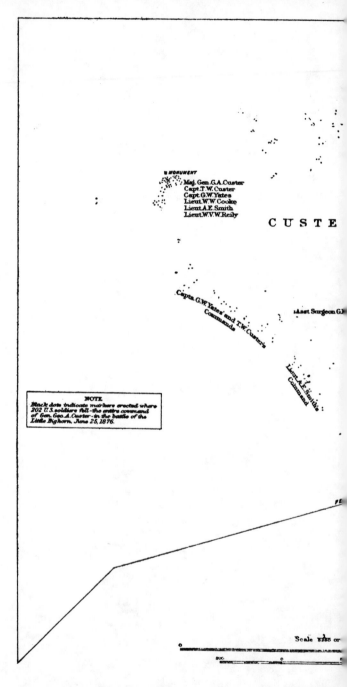

Plat showing the location of the graves on the Custer fie

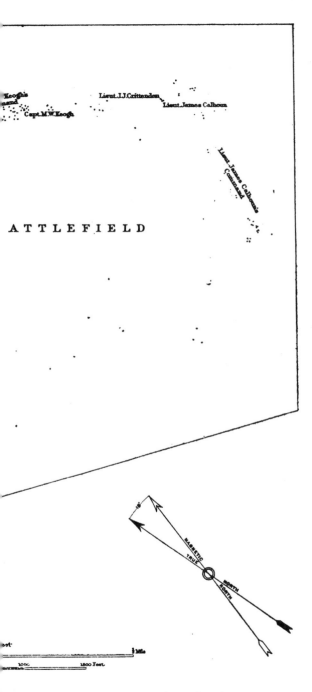

Keogh's
mend
Capt.M.W.Keogh

Lieut.J.J.Crittenden
Lieut.James Calhoun

Lieut. James Calhoun
Command

A T T L E F I E L D

MAGNETIC
TRUE

NORTH
SOUTH

½ Mile

1000   1800 Feet

he bodies were buried approximately where they fell.

JOURNAL

OF

THE MILITARY SERVICE INSTITUTION

OF THE

UNITED STATES.

" I cannot help plead to my countrymen, at every opportunity, to cherish all that is manly and noble in the military profession, because Peace is enervating and no man is wise enough to fore-tell when soldiers may be in demand again."—SHERMAN.

VOL. XVIII.   JANUARY, 1896.   NO. LXXIX.

THE CAMPAIGN AGAINST THE SIOUX IN 1876.

(From Official Sources.)

BY COLONEL ROBERT P. HUGHES, INSPECTOR GENERAL.

THE events which I am about to discuss occurred more than nineteen years ago. The central figure in them was General Terry, whose self-sacrificing charity and kindness of heart induced him to maintain unbroken silence in regard to them to the end of his life, except on rare, and in a sense confidential, occasions to a few intimate friends. Of these some are now dead, and certainly none are prepared, after such a lapse of time, to trust to memory alone for accuracy of statement. The official records are scattered and difficult to be obtained; some, known to have existed once, have disappeared and cannot now be found. Hence it can be readily understood that my determination to collect all the facts from authentic sources, in order to convincingly answer General Fry's comments on Captain Godfrey's story when they appeared in the *Century Magazine* for January, 1892, imposed a heavy task upon me; and, embarrassed as I was with the usual duties of my office, it was not accomplished without considerable delay. However, when the facts had been collected and properly arranged, they were presented to the editor of the *Century* in order that its readers might see both sides of the controversy and arrive at a just conclusion. The tender of my letter was not accepted.   I was informed that, if I reduced its length to the number of words in Fry's letter, it would then be accepted. Considering the fact that Fry started with Godfrey's tale as an extensive base from which to operate, that there were errors of fact in both productions to be corrected, and in addition to this the collated facts to be given, it will be readily understood that in fairness to the interests at stake, the terms offered could not be accepted.

It thus being impossible to reach the readers of the *Century*, and in consideration of the fact that such a statement, although compiled from official sources, must cause additional pain to those innocent souls who have already suffered more than enough, I determined to wait and see what the effect of the articles in the *Century* would be, and let this be the guide in my course of action.

In *Scribner's Magazine* for June, 1895, is an article from the pen of Dr. E. Benjamin Andrews, President of Brown University, entitled " A History of the Last Quarter-century," in which these two sentences appear :

"Some of General Terry's friends charged Custer with transgressing his orders in fighting as he did.   This has been disproved."

In response to an inquiry, Dr. Andrews writes me under date of July 3, 1895 :   " My statement in the *Scribner* is based on what Godfrey and Fry say in the *Century Magazine*.   Vol. pages 358–387."

I was not willing to believe that contemporary history would perpetuate error in this one-sided way, but I am now convinced that I failed in my duty to my friend and commander in not meeting the attacks at once; for it is now evident that the authentic facts should be placed where they may be accessible to the historian writing of that period.

It may, and probably will be said that heed should be given to the classic aphorism : *de mortuis nil nisi bonum.*   To this my reply is that it is not I who compel this presentation of facts. In common with many of General Terry's friends to whom they were known, I have paid due respect to his own charitable reticence.   The errors of Godfrey and Fry, now accepted by Andrews, make it obligatory on me to produce the facts in my possession.   The responsibility for their not being published before General Fry passed away rests with his own publishers.

Except to correct a few errors bearing on material facts, I shall leave Captain Godfrey's paper, which is the text for Fry's, to others. It does not nearly enough concern the matter in hand to make it necessary to remark upon his failure to state *all* of the well known facts.

Fry's lack of information will be made apparent in the compilation from the records which is to follow.

The question at issue arose from a statement made by Dr. T. T. Munger in his address at General Terry's funeral,—to the effect that the nobility of General Terry's character was finely illustrated in his conduct in withholding from the public the fact that Custer's disaster was in direct sequence to disobedience of orders, and that by his silence General Terry " suffered an imputation, hurtful to his military reputation, to rest on himself, rather than subject a brave but indiscreet subordinate to the charge of disobedience."

General Fry denies the truth of this assertion of disobedience and says that I deny having authorized Dr. Munger to make any use of my statement of the case to him, although I admit that I was probably the source from which he derived his information, and he reproaches me for failing to establish the fact of disobedience.

It is true that I did not authorize Dr. Munger to use my statement of that fact, and did not expect him to do so. But it is nevertheless true that Dr. Munger was fully justified by the facts in making the statement he did, and I shall show hereafter that this statement was exactly true.

The conversation which led to my mentioning the matter to Dr. Munger is, perhaps, scarcely pertinent, but it may not be amiss to briefly state it. I had gone to his house to see him on business, and was in the act of leaving him when he called me back by the remark and question : " You have been with General Terry for many years ; what do you consider to have been his chief characteristic as a man ? " My reply was spontaneous— " Self-sacrifice," and, in elucidation of that statement, I cited a series of incidents in which he had sunk all thought of self in consideration for others. Among them I referred to the Custer massacre and stated that, notwithstanding the fact that General Terry could not be held accountable for that terrible disaster, he had accepted the full responsibility rather than leave it with General Custer, who could not defend himself. I distinctly stated that General Custer had disobeyed General Terry's orders. The military events were not otherwise discussed. Our conversation on this occasion was short and this phase of it was distinctly limited to matters illustrative of the sacrifice General Terry made of himself at the time, and of his uniform and persistent silence ever afterwards under many and very trying provocations.

While I certainly did not expect Dr. Munger to make reference to that particular instance, given in elucidation of what I considered to be General Terry's most marked characteristic, still I wish to assume the full responsibility for my statement.

My position in the case has never been doubtful. I have stated it to others, and would have given the reasons for the belief that is in me to General Fry in person if he had ever suggested at any of our frequent meetings, while he was preparing his article, that he was seeking light upon the subject.

Dr. Andrews, in his letter of July 3d, referring to the two sentences above quoted, also says :

"I meant, however, by the accompanying statement, to imply what I suppose nearly all admit, that Custer was so bent on making a record that he was not duly attentive to the *spirit* of his orders."

The inconsistency between the two statements need not be remarked upon further than to say that by the latter the writer gives up his case, for it is a well understood principle in military orders of this character that the *spirit* is the sum and substance of the whole matter. In issuing orders like those in question, all authorities agree that the situation must be explained to the subordinate as it appears to the commander at the time of giving them, together with the plan and design, in order that the subordinate may exercise his intelligence and execute the "spirit" of his orders in case he finds it impossible, or unadvisable to follow them literally.

I now assume the task of showing that there was disobedience of orders.

The general story of the campaign is sufficiently well known to need no further recital of it except in so far as may be necessary to correct errors of fact in the statements made by the papers of Captain Godfrey and General Fry.

Although it is to be inferred from General Fry's comments that it was intended that General Terry's command should make a winter campaign and that Custer was prevented from moving by "bad weather," such is not the case.

The suggestion of a quick winter movement was made to

Sheridan by Terry, late in December, 1875. Terry had been in Chicago for a personal consultation with Sheridan, and, after returning to St. Paul, received from him, under date of December 20, 1875, the correspondence between the Interior and War Departments " for report as to the possibility of military operations against the hostile Indians named in the within report."

On the 28th of December, Terry reported that information, gathered from various sources, tended to show that these Indians were then encamped on the Little Missouri River, near its mouth and that, if that were true, it might be possible to strike them by a rapid movement from Fort Lincoln. But, in view of secrecy enjoined upon him in the matter, he had not even communicated with his staff on the subject, nor taken steps to ascertain the precise location of Sitting Bull's camp. He further asked approval of an effort to do this. This he got, and a little later, through Col. Huston, commanding Fort Stevenson, learned that "Sitting Bull and his band moved from the Little Missouri some time ago * * * and there are at present no camps of hostile or other Indians on that stream."

It was not until February 1, 1876, that the Secretary of the Interior informed the War Department that Sitting Bull, etc., refused to obey, and turned them over to be dealt with by the War Department. The matter was referred to the General of the Army, and on the 7th of February, to Sheridan, who, on February 8th sent it to Terry and duplicates to Crook, with instructions to commence hostilities. On February 8th, Terry telegraphed Sheridan : "Sitting Bull has left the Little Missouri and is now on the Yellowstone probably as high up as Powder River," to which Sheridan replied : " If Sitting Bull is not on the Little Missouri, as heretofore supposed to be, I am afraid but little can be done by you at this time."

February 17th, Terry communicated with Crook who replied March 1st from Fort Fetterman : " I hasten to answer before leaving here. The command under General Reynolds has already started. I expect to accompany the expedition so as to get some idea of the country and the difficulties to be overcome in a *summer campaign*. I hope to make this *scout* and get back before so using up my stock as to unfit them for a summer's campaign."*

On this "scout," General Crook encountered Crazy Horse,

---

* The italics are my own.—R. P. H.

was repulsed and returned. It is clear that there was no order to Custer to move, which Fry asserts existed, and therefore nothing could result from his "inability to move." On the contrary, Terry writes Gibbon, under date of February 21st: "I expect to start Custer about the 1st of April," and, about the same time, explained his plan to Sheridan: "*I think my only plan will be to give Custer a secure base well up on the Yellowstone from which he can operate, at which he can find supplies, and to which he can retire in case at any time the Indians gather in too great numbers for the small force which he will have.*" * For this purpose he proposed to send six companies of infantry and asked for *steamboat* transportation for them, clearly showing that there was no purpose to move Custer before navigation opened, which would be April at the very earliest, and most probably a month later. From this time on, preparations continued, all directed to this plan, which contemplated Custer's going in command as indicated.

Fry attributes the accession to the Sitting Bull and Crazy Horse forces from the agency early in the spring to the "repulse of Crook's column, and the inability of Custer to move." It is shown that Crook's movement was merely a scout, and that no movement by Custer had been intended, and if Fry knew anything of Indian habits, he would have known what Terry and Crook both knew and calculated upon, that with the opening of spring there would be large desertions from the agencies to the hostiles, chiefly of fighting men. Neither of the causes assigned by him for this, had they existed, would have seriously affected this fact.

Fry then says: "It *happened* that while the expedition was being fitted out, Custer *unwittingly* incurred the displeasure of President Grant, who directed that Custer should not accompany the column. Through his appeal to the President and the intercession of Terry *and Sheridan*, Custer was permitted to go in command of his regiment, but Terry was *required* to accompany and command the column."

The statement that "Custer *unwittingly* incurred the displeasure of President Grant who thereupon directed that he should be deprived of his command," attributes to President Grant conduct and motives little in accord with his well-known character. Is it possible that President Grant would have arbitrarily interposed his high office to humiliate an officer, and deprive him of his rights, for any reason that could be so little gravity as that the officer had "*unwittingly* incurred his displeasure"? Not many of our people will believe that of Grant, and how far it was from true is shown by the telegrams from Sheridan to Sherman which follow. The latter part of the statement that "Custer was permitted to go, but Terry was *required* to accompany and command the column," conveys an implication of reluctance on Terry's part to go that is very wide of the facts. As will be seen, it was originally intended that Custer should command one of the columns. When he was ordered to be relieved and forbidden to go, the question of who should be substituted for him was discussed between Terry and Sheridan, ending in the latter's telegraphing:

"*The names you suggest are very good, but I believe the command will be better satisfied in having the Department Commander in charge.*"

This is the first intimation of the idea of Terry's going.

To this Terry instantly replied:

"*Your dispatch received. I will go myself.*"

Subsequently, as will be noted, Terry, in interceding for Custer, gives strength to his plea for him in saying:

"*Whether Lieutenant Colonel Custer shall be permitted to accompany my column or not, I shall go in command of it.*"

These telegrams make it very clear that Fry's assertion that "Custer was permitted to go, but Terry was *required* to accompany," does not accurately present the facts either in statement or implication.

It is to be understood that Terry held it to be unadvisable for a Department Commander to abandon the reins of his department—and that was what it amounted to—in order to take command in person of a minor portion of his troops in the field. He always insisted that such opportunities for interesting service belonged as a matter of right to those officers whose rank corresponded with the command employed.

This brings me to the necessary reproduction of the correspondence (chiefly telegraphic) which gives the history of Custer's being relieved from the command Terry contemplated giving him, and his subsequent re-instatement in command of his own regiment.

March 15th, Terry received at St. Paul from Custer at Fort Lincoln a telegram:

"I am just in receipt of a summons from the Sergeant-at-Arms of the House directing me to appear forthwith. I will telegraph and endeavor to

avoid going. Should I be forced to go must I obtain an order from Department Headquarters, or what course must I pursue?"

To which Terry replied:

"You need no order beyond the summons of the Committee. I am
sorry to have you go for I fear it will delay our movements. I should suppose that if your testimony is not to the facts, themselves, and will only
point out to the committee the witnesses from whom they can get the
facts, your information might be communicated by letter or by telegraph,
and that being done you might ask to be relieved from personal attendance
without exposing yourself to any misconstruction."

To this Custer sent two replies on the 16th—the first:

"Acting on your suggestion I have sent long telegram to chairman of
committee requesting to be allowed to testify here and forward by mail."

And later:

"After further consideration fearing my request to be relieved from
obeying summons might be misconstrued into a desire to avoid testifying
I have concluded to prefer no request to that effect."

March 24th, Custer passed through St. Paul en route to Washington. He remained in Washington until May 2d. Meantime,
April 20th, he telegraphed from Washington to St. Paul that he
left that day " en route for St. Paul, stopping at Detroit under
orders," and April 24th from New York: " Intended leaving here
to day for St. Paul but have been this moment summoned by
Sergeant-at-Arms of Senate to appear at impeachment trial on
Thursday. I will leave Washington at earliest moment practicable," and on the same day again telegraphed Terry from New
York:

"When I left Washington it was with the understanding with the impeachment managers that I would probably not be required on impeachment trial, but that I should return to Lincoln, and if necessary would be
summoned by telegraph. This was after I had made repeated requests to
be discharged and to be permitted to return to my post. The summons
was a complete surprise to me. I still believe I will be able to get away
from Washington this week, the chances being against a trial on grounds of
want of jurisdiction, and if the trial takes place it is extremely doubtful if
my testimony will be desired. I have strongly represented to the managers
the necessity for my presence with my command. I wish you would telegraph me Arlington House at Washington stating the approaching readiness of expedition and the desirability of my presence at Lincoln. I think
with that I can induce the managers to permit me to go at once. My absence from my command is wholly against my desire."

And again the same day :

"The Secretary of War will address a communication to impeachment managers to-day representing the importance of the duties at Lincoln in connection with expedition and requesting that I be permitted to return at the earliest practicable date."

Sheridan telegraphed Terry April 28th :

" The General of the Army telegraphs me that instructions have been received through the Secretary of War coming from the President to send some one other than Custer in charge of the expedition from Fort Lincoln. I wish to consult you as to whom you wish to go in command so as to submit the name to the General of the Army for detail."

Terry replied on same day :

" The officers available at present in the Department are Crittenden 17th and Sykes 20th. Crittenden is senior to Sykes and has intimated a desire for such duty. Reno would like the command but his rank seems to be insufficient, so long as colonels are available. Hazen of the 6th writes me from New York that he expects to return soon to his post, and that he desires useful service, should there be opportunity for him, but that he is summoned to Washington by investigating committee. He is senior to both Crittenden and Sykes but I suppose that he is not immediately available. I propose Crittenden."

Sheridan replied the next day (29th) :

" After a careful consideration of the situation I think the best way to meet it, and that promising the most satisfaction and the greatest success would be for you to go yourself. The names you suggest are very good but I believe the command will be better satisfied in having the Department Commander in charge."

To this Terry replied at once :

" Your dispatch received. I will go myself."

On the same day Custer telegraphed from Washington to Terry :

"Confidential. I telegraphed you yesterday that Secretary Taft would address a communication to impeachment managers looking to my early return to my command. The suggestion was made to Secretary through General Sherman. The Secretary stated to General Sherman he would write the letter after Cabinet meeting, but at the latter he mentioned his intention to the President who directed him not to write the impeachment managers requesting my discharge, but to substitute some other officer to command expedition. I saw Sherman's dispatch and the reply to Sheridan. I at once sought an interview with the managers of impeachment and obtained from them authority to leave. Would have started this evening but General Sherman suggested that I delay until Monday in order to see the President."

And also on the same day :

" I leave Monday for Fort Lincoln for duty with my command, authority to do so having been granted to-day."

On May 1st, Custer telegraphed Terry from Washington:

"At my request order directing me to return via Detroit revoked. I expect to reach St. Paul Friday."

On May 3d, Terry received the following telegram from General Sheridan's headquarters:

"The Lieutenant General directs me to transmit to you the following telegram from the General of the Army for your information and action:

"Gen. P. H. Sheridan, Chicago, Illinois.

"I am at this moment advised that General Custer started last night for St. Paul and Fort Abraham Lincoln. He was not justified in leaving without seeing the President and myself. Please intercept him and await further orders; meantime let the expedition proceed without him.

(Signed) "W. T. Sherman, General."

"Should Lieutenant Colonel Custer not be intercepted here you will take such steps as will secure his detention at St. Paul until further orders are received from higher authority.

(Signed) "R. C. Drum."

On May 4th, Custer telegraphed Terry from Chicago:

"I have just forwarded the following dispatch, and a second one asking that after the first has been considered I be authorized to proceed to Fort Lincoln. I was in the St. Paul train when General Sheridan's staff officer informed me that the General desired to see me."

"Chicago, Ill., May 4th, 1876.

"Gen. W. T. Sherman, Washington.

"I have seen your dispatch to General Sheridan directing me to await orders here and am at a loss to understand that portion referring to my departure from Washington without seeing you or the President as I called at the White House at 10 A. M. on Monday, sent my card to the President and with the exception of a few minutes' absence at the War Department I remained at the White House awaiting an audience with the President until 3 P. M, when he sent me word that he could not see me. I called at your office at about 2 P. M., but was informed by Col. McCook that you had not returned from New York but were expected in the evening. I called at your hotel at 4 P. M., and about 6 P. M., but was informed by the clerk that you had not returned from New York. I requested Colonel McCook to inform you of the substance of the above and also that I was to leave at seven that evening to join my command. While at the War Department that day I also reported the fact of my proposed departure to the Adjutant General and the Inspector General of the Army and obtained from them written and verbal authority to proceed to my command without visiting Detroit as previously ordered to do. At my last interview with you, I informed you that I would leave Washington Monday night to join my command, and you in conversation replied that it was the best thing I could do; besides you frequently during my stay in Washington called my attention to the necessity of my leaving as soon as possible.

(Signed) " G. A. Custer."

On the same day (May 4th), Custer sent Terry four other telegrams:

"Telegram just received from Sherman states orders have been sent to Sheridan to order me to proceed to Lincoln on duty. I leave in the morning for St. Paul."

Again:

" When will you start from Lincoln ?* I am hoping to obtain an early decision in my case from Washington. Sheridan has no information further than that contained in Sherman's two dispatches to him both of which you have seen."

Again:

" I will reach St. Paul to-morrow morning. No decided change since my last dispatch. Will be better understood after interview than by telegraphing details."

Again:

" I still hope that after seeing you the present restrictions may be removed."

On the 5th, Terry received the following telegram from headquarters in Chicago:

" The Lieutenant General directs me to transmit for your information and guidance the following telegram from the General of the Army:

" ' Have just come from the President who orders that General Custer be allowed to rejoin his post, to remain there on duty, but not to accompany the expedition supposed to be on the point of starting against the hostile Indians under General Terry.

Signed)　　　" ' W. T. Sherman, General.'

" ' Please acknowledge receipt.　　　(Signed)　　R. C. Drum.' "

On May 6th, Terry telegraphed Sheridan:

" At Lieutenant Colonel Custer's request I telegraph that he arrived here, and reported for duty this morning."

An analysis of the preceding correspondence shows that while the preparations were in progress for the Custer column to leave about April or May from Fort Abraham Lincoln, Custer was summoned to Washington by the Sergeant-at-Arms of the House of Representatives to testify in the Belknap impeachment case ; that he went with some reluctance; that, after reaching Washington, he endeavored to be discharged from the summons and

---

* The expedition was to start from Lincoln.

return to his command; that, when finally permitted to disregard the House summons, he was almost immediately summoned by the Committee of the Senate; that he endeavored to be discharged from that summons; that, to this end, he sought the aid of the Secretary of War, who consulted the President and was directed not to write to the Committee, but to substitute some officer for Custer in command; that, when this came to the knowledge of Custer, he saw the impeachment committee in person and obtained their permission to leave; that thereupon, in two or three days, he did leave Washington and in this, as expressed by General Sherman, he "was not justified without seeing the President and myself," and was followed by telegraphic orders to Sheridan at Chicago to intercept and detain him; that this was subsequently modified into allowing him to go to Fort Lincoln for duty, but not to accompany the expedition.

It would seem to be impossible for an unbiassed mind to conclude that the foregoing correspondence rested on no other foundation than the displeasure of President Grant "unwittingly incurred."

The causes, alleged at the time, for relieving Custer from command of the expeditionary column had no bearing on, or connection with the campaign of 1876; they related to the operations of a previous year, and it is needless to say that they did not touch the President in any way.

General Custer himself is my authority for stating that, while in Chicago, he endeavored to interest the Lieutenant General in the affair and to secure his intercession with the President in his behalf, but Sheridan declined to do anything in the matter.

Custer then came to St. Paul under orders to go to Fort Lincoln and there remain. Here was still another resort—and it was the last—between him and what he himself denominated "humiliation." This lay in the well-known generosity of General Terry. Custer sought his interposition—how earnestly is testified by General Terry's own words later used to a few persons of whom some are still living:

"Custer * * * and with tears in his eyes, begged my aid. How could I resist it?"

Terry yielded to these pleas and wrote and sent the following dispatch, of which *every word* (including what is signed as Custer's) *was his own composition:*

" Headquarters Department of Dakota,
"St. Paul, Minn., May 6th, 1876.
" The Adjutant General,
" Division of the Missouri, Chicago.
" I forward the following :
" 'To His Excellency, the President :
(Through Military Channels).

" 'I have seen your order transmitted through the General of the Army directing that I be not permitted to accompany the expedition to move against the hostile Indians. As my entire regiment forms a part of the expedition and as I am the senior officer of the regiment on duty in this department I respectfully but most earnestly request that while not allowed to go in command of the expedition I may be permitted to serve with my regiment in the field. I appeal to you as a soldier to spare me the humiliation of seeing my regiment march to meet the enemy and I not to share its dangers. (Signed) G. A. Custer.' "

" In forwarding the above I wish to say, expressly, that I have no desire whatever to question the orders of the President or of my military superiors. Whether Lieutenant Colonel Custer shall be permitted to accompany the column or not I shall go in command of it. I do not know the reasons upon which the orders given rest ; but if these reasons do not forbid it, Lieutenant Colonel Custer's services would be very valuable with his regiment. (Signed) Alfred H. Terry,
" Commanding Department."

This was forwarded as indicated through Terry's military superiors and was endorsed by Sheridan as follows :

"Chicago, Illinois, May 7th, 1876.
" Brigadier General E. D. Townsend,
" Washington, D. C.

" The following dispatch from General Terry is respectfully forwarded. I am sorry Lieutenant Colonel Custer did not manifest as much interest in staying at his post to organize and get ready his regiment and the expedition as he now does to accompany it. On a previous occasion in eighteen sixty-eight I asked executive clemency for Colonel Custer to enable him to accompany his regiment against the Indians, and I sincerely hope that if granted this time it may have sufficient effect to prevent him from again attempting to throw discredit upon his profession and his brother officers. (Signed) " P. H. Sheridan, Lieutenant General."

The result is shown by the following dispatch from Sherman :

" Headquarters of the Army,
" Washington, May 8th, 1876.
" To General A. H. Terry, St. Paul, Minn. :
" General Sheridan's enclosing yours of yesterday touching General

Custer's urgent request to go under your command with his regiment has been submitted to the President, who sent me word that if you want General Custer along he withdraws his objections. Advise Custer to be prudent, not to take along any newspaper men, who always make mischief, and to abstain from personalities in the future. * * *

(Signed) " W. T. SHERMAN,

"General."

The result of Terry's intercession (hardly of Terry *and Sheridan's*—as Fry states it) and of his determination to take him " along " was communicated to Custer by General Terry on the morning of May 8th at the headquarters of the Department of Dakota, corner of Wabashaw and 4th Streets, St. Paul, Minn.

From this interview Custer proceeded to his hotel—the Metropolitan—a few blocks away, and en route he encountered Colonel Ludlow of the Engineer Corps of the U. S. Army. To this officer he related the fact that he was restored to the command of his regiment and was to accompany General Terry's column, and added a statement that his purpose would be at the first chance in the campaign to " cut loose from (and make his operations independent of) General Terry during the summer "; that he had " got away with Stanley and would be able to swing clear of Terry."

Under the peculiar circumstances, this announcement could not have been made earlier than late in the morning of the 8th. Ludlow repeated Custer's remarks to Colonel Farquhar, Corps of Engineers, U. S. A., General Ruggles, A. A. G., U. S. A., and General Card, Chief Quartermaster of the Department, not later than 10 A. M. on the morning of the 9th. Terry, with his staff and Custer, had taken an early train that morning for Fort Lincoln to join the mobilized troops. Ludlow's purpose was that this information should be conveyed to General Terry, and General Ruggles fully intended to communicate it, and still thinks that he wrote a letter giving the information. But whether it escaped his mind in the great press of public business in his office, or the letter was lost en route to its destination, after trustworthy and regular means of communication were cut off, has not been and probably never will be determined.

Colonel Ludlow had just been ordered to Philadelphia and his position on the staff was taken by Lieutenant Maguire. It thus happened that the above-mentioned announcement of the intention did not come to the knowledge of Terry until his return to St. Paul the last of September, and until then Colonel Ludlow was not called upon to remember the exact words which Custer used, and, while these exact words may have faded from his memory, the idea conveyed to him was still perfectly clear and was given by him, as above quoted, in a letter to General Terry.

All of these officers agree as to the character of the remark made by Custer to Ludlow as given within a few hours after it was made.

Such a statement, made at that time by Custer to a brother officer, has very significant relation to subsequent events.

Setting aside the revelation which it makes of his ingratitude to the man to whose kindness he had just owed his restoration to command, which is not under consideration, it goes far to explain his conduct on the first occasion when he got the chance "to swing clear of Terry." To this relation of it I will revert later.

Terry, accompanied by his staff and Custer, arrived at Fort Lincoln on the night of the 10th, assumed command of the mobilized column on the 14th, and marched out with it on the 17th.

It is not necessary to discuss the intermediate events of the campaign until the time immediately preceding the massacre. But it is best at this point to correct statements made by Fry.

From Sherman's report he quotes: "Up to the moment of Custer's defeat, there was nothing, official or private, to justify an officer to expect that any detachment would encounter more than 500 or 800 warriors," and otherwise asserts that everybody greatly underestimated the Indian strength.

That the strength finally found was greater than was believed possible is true, but that the disparity was such as Sherman asserts and Fry states is far from the fact.

As early as February 16th Terry wrote Division Headquarters as follows:

> "I earnestly request that the three companies of the 7th Cavalry now serving in the Department of the Gulf may be ordered to rejoin their regiment in this department. The orders which have been given recently render indispensably necessary a larger mounted force than the nine companies of the 7th now in this department. These nine companies comprise but six hundred and twenty men all told, and of these not over five hundred and fifty could be put into the field for active operations. This number is not sufficient for the end in view. For if the Indians who pass the winter in the Yellowstone and Powder rivers country should be found gathered in one camp, or in contiguous camps (and they usually are so gathered) they could not be attacked by that number without great risk of defeat. * * * "

Finally these companies were sent him.

At this date Terry believed Sitting Bull's personal following to be about five hundred lodges, which means many more than that number of fighting men. He and every one else familiar with the matter, knew that Sitting Bull was only one of the many disaffected chiefs, each with his personal following or band, and that, with the first opening of spring, important accessions of young, ambitious, restless bucks would be received from the agencies on the Missouri. Such telegrams as the following, sent by Terry to Division Headquarters on Christmas eve, 1875, were familiar to all concerned in those days :

" Capt. Poland telegraphs that, although there is no game in the vicinity, the Indians at Standing Rock are selling all their hides for ammunition. These Indians are closely connected with Sitting Bull's band, and, having in view the recent conversation of the Lieutenant General with me, and the communication of the Interior Department to the War Department, which was referred to me on the 20th instant, I have ordered Poland to put a stop to such sales. I suggest that the Interior Department be requested to give similar orders to the trader."

March 24th, Terry telegraphed Sheridan again urgently asking for the troops in Louisiana, and added :

" The most trustworthy scout on the Missouri recently in hostile camp reports not less than two thousand lodges and that the Indians are loaded down with ammunition."

April 1st, Custer telegraphed the report of scout Reynolds that

" From three hundred to six hundred lodges under Sitting Bull are now en route to Berthold."*

May 14th, Terry, on the eve of starting, telegraphed Sheridan from Fort Lincoln :

" It is represented that they have fifteen hundred lodges, are confident and intend making a stand."

While the following was not in Terry's possession before the fight, it seems to show that Sheridan had confirmation of Terry's last dispatch to him from Fort A. Lincoln :

" Chicago, June 6th.

" Courier from Red Cloud agency reported at Laramie yesterday that Yellow Robe arrived at agency (six days from hostile camp). He says that

---

* NOTE.—Scout Reynolds had been sent by Custer to ascertain the situation with orders to report to him personally, hence the report had gone to Custer in Washington.

eighteen hundred lodges* were on the Rosebud and about to leave for Powder river, below the point of Crazy Horse's fight, and says they will fight and have about three thousand warriors. This is sent for your information.

(Signed)   " M. V. SHERIDAN."

All this shows that no such ridiculously inadequate estimate of the number as "500 to 800 warriors" was in the minds of the responsible heads, and wholly negatives the statement from Sherman, quoted and relied upon by Fry. Had the latter possessed even the small knowledge of Indian matters which he discredits Terry with possessing, he would not have allowed himself to be betrayed by Sherman's statement (which was made when discussing another matter, and apparently without a full consideration of the facts), and would have been sure that Terry was always fully aware that his troops were dealing not only with hostiles estimated at from 500 to 800, but with the available part of the agency Indians, who had gone out to help their friends in a fight.

According to Godfrey, Custer himself stated in terms that they would have to face three times that number.

That General Custer was made aware of the unprecedented size of the Indian village before leaving the divide between the Rosebud and the Little Big Horn is quite certain. Captain Hare, 7th Cavalry, who was on duty with the scouts, says: "I heard Mitch Bouyer myself tell General Custer that it was the largest village that had ever collected in the Northwest, and that he, Bouyer, had been with those Indians for many years, over thirty I think he said." This was after Mitch Bouyer, *et al*, had shown Custer the enormous pony herd from the Crow's Nest, and before he, Custer, had divided his command.

As the question of the number of warriors in the hostile camp has been raised, it may not be amiss to recall an incident that took place on the hill, on which Reno took refuge, within a few minutes after General Terry's arrival. He and some of the

---

* This telegram is the only one to which I can trace Godfrey's statement that " Information was dispatched from General Sheridan that *from one agency alone* about eighteen hundred lodges had set out to join the hostile camp ; but that information did not reach General Terry until several days after the battle." It can be seen that this telegram fails to support the statement, and I can find no other that will justify it in any degree. In this Sheridan speaks of the united hostile camp, and not of deserters from agencies, or " from one agency alone." It is utter nonsense to intimate that General Sheridan considered it possible that eighteen hundred lodges had set out from any one agency to join the hostiles.

officers of his staff were surrounded by a group of officers of the 7th Cavalry amongst whom were Major Reno, Colonel Benteen, Colonel Weir and Major Moylan,—all officers of long and varied experience in the army. General Terry put the direct question to them: "What is your estimate of the number of the Indian warriors?" The replies pivoted about the figure 1500, and I can recall Colonel Benteen's reply almost verbatim which was as follows: "I have been accustomed to seeing divisions of cavalry during the war, and from my observations I would say that there were from fifteen to eighteen hundred warriors." No one in the group at that time, put this estimate above eighteen hundred.

The gist of this discussion, however, is found in Fry's attempt to controvert the statement that "Custer's fatal movement was in direct violation of orders." In attempting this he begins with an assumption which has no warrant whatever, and which is plainly contradicted by facts. Fry says: "But it is highly probable that the 'plan' when Custer moved had neither the force nor importance which it subsequently acquired in Terry's mind." In support of this pure assumption, Fry points out that Terry's "full and explicit report June 27th when the subject was fresh, in which he spoke of the conference but did not say or intimate that a plan of operations had been decided upon in it," and that it was "not until July 2d that he reported the existence of a plan."

The history of these two reports is and has been well known for many years, and if Fry did not know the facts, it certainly was not because they were not public property.

In brief, that history is as follows: The report of June 27th was written by General Terry on the field immediately upon his getting a full knowledge of the facts of the disaster. It was sent with all possible speed by a special courier ("Muggins" Taylor) to Fort Ellis and Bozeman, Montana (the latter being the nearest telegraph station, and supposed to be the quickest mode of communication), to be sent from the first point at which the telegraph line in operation might be reached.* The dispatch was written late in the day, June 27th, when all the horrors of the disaster had fully appeared to him. Before sending it, Terry read it to a group of his staff officers by the light of a candle. It is within the knowledge of Captain (now Major) H. J. Now-

---

* The line was frequently broken in those days by buffalo rubbing down the poles.

lan, 7th Cavalry, and myself, as two of the members who made up that group,* that, after hearing it read, there was a spontaneous and earnest protest made by the assembled officers against excluding the fact that disobedience had occurred and had caused the miscarriage of a well-considered plan that promised a great success, and that the failure of the campaign was fairly attributable to this want of loyalty in one of his subordinates.

Fry characterizes this report as "full and explicit," and, on Terry's omission to make any mention in it of the plan, and of Custer's disobedience, he bases much of what he says to Terry's discredit about the plan's being an after-thought. I will return to this point later, only wishing now to say this:

This report was as "full and explicit" as was consistent with General Terry's purpose, avowed at the time, and adhered to in spite of the remonstrances of his staff officers, that he would not give to the public the fact that Custer had flagrantly disobeyed, but would rather himself "bear an imputation hurtful to his military reputation."

After dispatching this report to Lieutenant General Sheridan and in the belief that it would be the first knowledge of the disaster that would reach the outside world, General Terry devoted all his energies and resources to the burial of the dead, care of the wounded and in providing means for, and transporting them to the steamer *Far West,* in order that they might be sent as quickly as possible to Fort Lincoln, many hundred miles away to be covered by very doubtful river navigation.

This once accomplished, and the steamer at the mouth of the Big Horn in readiness to leave under charge of Captain E. W. Smith of his staff, Terry prepared in haste and sent by the hands of Smith the second report—that of July 2d—which was to be transmitted to Lieutenant General Sheridan from Bismarck, which was the first point at which he could reach a telegraph line. One very important fact must not be overlooked: This second report (of July 2d) was distinctly marked and made "Confidential" by Terry, and the original rough draft of it is in my possession now and doubters can see it for themselves. All necessary precautions were supposed to have been taken to prevent this dispatch from going to the public. By the unanticipated event that the

---

* But three of the nine officers composing the headquarters group are now living. The third is Lieutenant (now Captain) R. E. Thompson, Signal Corps. I have not inquired whether he was present or not.

telegraph line was down and the special courier who carried the report of June 27th failed to get his dispatch on the wires east of Helena, coupled with the fact that the steamer *Far West* (owing to the energy of Grant Marsh, Master, and the swift current due to the unusual stage of water) made the trip down to Bismarck with unprecedented celerity and success, the "Confidential" report was the first to reach its destination and the first one received from Terry by any one, and contained the earliest authentic information of the events to which it referred. This dispatch was immediately forwarded to General Sheridan and given by him to General Sherman, both of whom were then in Philadelphia, still kept strictly "confidential" and never intended to be otherwise. General Sherman received it in Philadelphia, and wishing to transmit it to the Secretary of War by telegraph, unfortunately entrusted it to a young man whom he supposed to be a proper messenger, but who proved to be an enterprising newspaper reporter who availed himself of the opportunity, copied the dispatch and gave it to the public press. Thus it came about that Terry's self-sacrificing purpose, formed on the field of disaster, and ever after during his life firmly adhered to,— to keep from the public all knowledge of the open disobedience of his dead subordinate, and bear himself all the probable consequent criticism (all the more trying because unjust), was in part defeated, and that result now makes it possible for ill-disposed critics to use the two dispatches to sustain the proposition that the importance of the "plan" was in point of fact an afterthought, a bastard conception originating through a desire on Terry's part to avoid blame. An assumption more at variance with the truth of the matter could hardly be conceived.

That it is absolutely unwarranted is again put beyond question through a letter still existing written by General Terry to his sisters from the mouth of the Rosebud on the evening of June 21st, before Custer's column started. This letter indulges in personalities foreign to the matter in question, and is not reproduced here, but in it he relates the events of the past ten days and then explains his plan, closing the subject with the remark "I have considerable hope that this combined movement may justify the expedition."

This brings us to the examination of the claim that Custer's written orders permitted him to do what he did.

Courtesy of phraseology in an order takes nothing from its

force, and the conditions being found as supposed, and the definite purpose of the commander being certainly known, nothing, save the most dire necessity, will justify the subordinate in departing in any way from his instructions. Even then the subordinate must look for protection against charges of disobedience to the fact that his judgment of the course pursued by him will be sustained and confirmed by other judgments that must pass upon his conduct. Even when some discretion is given to the subordinate to meet unanticipated events in his own way, he is still responsible that the way he takes is in entire accord with the "spirit" of his instructions, and as nearly as may be with the expressed will (desire) of the commander.

Fry italicizes, as if giving full discretion to Custer, the phrase in Terry's order: "*It is, of course, impossible to give you any definite instructions in regard to this movement.*" If this stood by itself it might possibly fairly admit of that construction, but as a matter of fact it is immediately followed by a much more pregnant and definite sentence to which Fry gives no attention whatever, and so may lead the unwary reader to regard it as of no moment, to wit: "*He will, however, indicate to you his own views of what your action should be, and he desires that you should conform to them unless you shall see sufficient reason for departing from them.*"

All military men know that the polite words "he desires," "he thinks," have all the force that can be conveyed in the words "he orders."

It may be well to explain that General Crook with a column of troops was to leave Fort Fetterman about the time General Terry's column would reach the Little Missouri River, which was conceded to be the first stream on which the Indians might possibly be found; that upon reaching that stream, and thereafter, Terry endeavored to sweep the country southward far enough to touch the field of Crook's operations, and thus assure himself that no bands of Indians were left in his rear. Pursuant to this system, Major Reno was detached from the camp on the Powder on the 10th of June with six companies of the 7th Cavalry to examine the Powder River Valley as far up as the mouth of the Little Powder, thence west to the Mizpah, and down that stream to its mouth and down the Tongue to its confluence with the Yellowstone, at which point he would then find General Terry with the balance of the command.

After getting out of range of the Department Commander, Major Reno, in violation of his instructions, bolted straight for the Rosebud, which he struck near its mouth. He found the oft-mentioned trail and followed it for some distance and then returned without having accomplished his mission, which was to ascertain whether there were any Indians on the Powder, Tongue, etc.

Reno did not pursue the trail he found far enough to determine in which direction it finally turned. It was possible, though not considered probable, that it would turn to the eastward. So true was this that we find General Custer instructing the commander of his scouts to watch constantly for trails leading east from the Rosebud. This being the case, it can be readily seen that absolute, or "definite instructions," were not only "impossible," but would have been utterly inconsistent with the situation.

Fry continues: "The order Custer received was to 'proceed up the Rosebud in pursuit of the Indians.' Surely he did not disobey that. Everything else was left to his discretion. As Terry did not wish to hamper Custer's action when nearly in contact with the enemy, and found it impossible to give him precise orders, plainly Custer did not, could not, disobey orders in any blamable sense, and plainly, also, he was expected to come 'in contact with the enemy.'"

In other words, according to Fry's version, the only order Custer had was to "proceed up the Rosebud in pursuit of the Indians." That this is a grave misconception of the facts becomes apparent from an examination of the map in connection with the order.

The Indian encampment was believed to lie to the north of the Big Horn Mountains, east of and near the Big Horn River, in the valley of the Little Big Horn River; but it was considered possible that it was located on the Rotten Grass, which was one day's march further up the Big Horn River. The Big Horn runs almost directly north. The immense snow-fields of the Big Horn Mountains fill all these streams, and during the hot days of early summer a great volume of water pours down them. The incline of the bed of the Big Horn is so great that when the channel is full, as it usually is in the month of June, the stream is practically impassable. It is thus seen that the Indian position could only be approached from the north or east. If a concentrated attack were made from the north, a line of escape was left open to the eastward. General Terry's " Plan " was for Custer's column, which was the strategic one of his command, to occupy this eastward line and so cut off escape in that direction before the Indians were disturbed, while Gibbon's column closed in from the north. In order to effect this " combined movement," and secure joint action as speedily as possible, it was very important that Gibbon should be informed of the situation at the head of Tullock's Fork, and of Custer's discoveries and consequent movements. The instructions to Custer are here reproduced *in extenso :*

Camp at Mouth of Rosebud River, Montana Territory,
June 22d, 1876.
Lieutenant-Colonel Custer,
7th Cavalry.
Colonel :

The Brigadier-General Commanding directs that, as soon as your regiment can be made ready for the march, you will proceed up the Rosebud in pursuit of the Indians whose trail was discovered by Major Reno a few days since. It is, of course, impossible to give you any definite instructions in regard to this movement, and were it not impossible to do so the Department Commander places too much confidence in your zeal, energy, and ability to wish to impose upon you precise orders which might hamper your action when nearly in contact with the enemy. He will, however, indicate to you his own views of what your action should be, and he desires that you should conform to them unless you shall see sufficient reasons for departing from them. He thinks that you should proceed up the Rosebud until you ascertain definitely the direction in which the trail above spoken of leads. Should it be found (as it appears almost certain that it will be found) to turn towards the Little Horn,* he thinks that you should still proceed southward, perhaps as far as the headwaters of the Tongue, and then turn towards the Little Horn, feeling constantly, however, to your left, so as to preclude the possibility of the escape of the Indians to the south or southeast by passing around your left flank. The column of Colonel Gibbon is now in motion for the mouth of the Big Horn. As soon as it reaches that point it will cross the Yellowstone and move up at least as far as the forks of the Big and Little Horns. Of course its future movements must be controlled by circumstances as they arise, but it is hoped that the Indians, if upon the Little Horn, may be so nearly inclosed by the two columns that their escape will be impossible.

The Department Commander desires that on your way up the Rosebud you should thoroughly examine the upper part of Tulloch's Creek, and that you should endeavor to send a scout through to Colonel Gibbon's column, with information of the result of your examination. The lower part of this

---

* At the time this was written, it was not generally understood that the full Indian appellation of this stream was Little Big Horn. R. P. H.

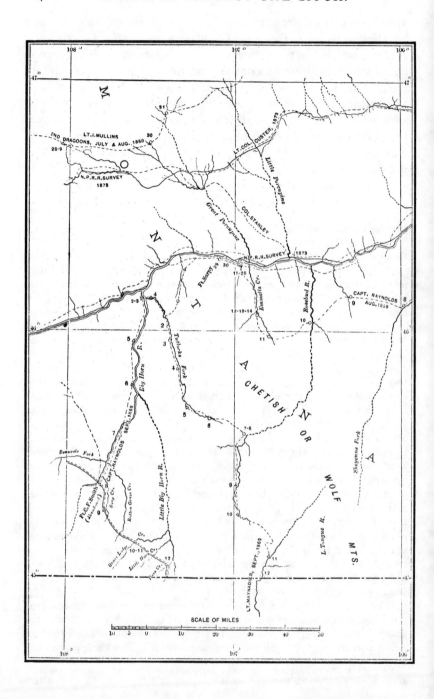

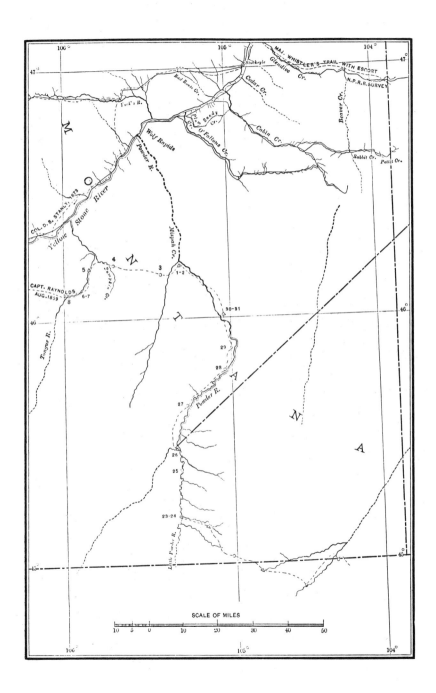

creek will be examined by a detachment from Colonel Gibbon's command. The supply steamer will be pushed up the Big Horn as far as the forks if the river is found to be navigable for that distance, and the Department Commander, who will accompany the column of Colonel Gibbon, desires you to report to him there not later than the expiration of the time for which your troops are rationed, unless in the meantime you receive further orders.

Very respectfully, your obedient servant,

E. W. Smith,

Captain 18th Infantry,

Acting Assistant Adjutant General."

As Captain Godfrey says, and rightly, " these instructions are explicit, and fixed the location of the Indians very accurately."

In view of all the facts, now so well known, it is difficult to know how Terry could have been more explicit in orders, more definite in purpose, and more clearly prescient of what Custer would find on his march. Subsequent knowledge shows conclusively that Terry's reasoning concerning the movements and locality of the Indians, from such information as he was then able to obtain, was marvellously correct, and that, as will be shown later, the " plan," which was based on the conclusions then drawn, was logically sound and professionally complete, and would, probably, have been crowned with success if it had been loyally adhered to.

It is first to inquire exactly what Custer's orders were, and then to determine how far he was entrusted with discretion to deviate from them.

A concise summary of what was explicit and positive in his orders presents : That Custer was to go up the Rosebud, following the Indian trail discovered by Reno a few days before, until he should ascertain definitely the direction in which it led. Should he find (" as it appears almost certain that it will be found ") that the trail turned towards the Little Big Horn, he should still proceed southward perhaps as far south as the headwaters of the Tongue, and then (and not till then) turn towards the Little Big Horn.

Then follows the definite explanation (already well understood by Custer through the conferences held during the afternoon of the 21st) of the coöperative prospective movements of Gibbon's command, and of Terry's hope that thus the Indians, if upon the Little Big Horn, might be so nearly inclosed by the two columns that their escape would be impossible. He was further ordered that, on the way up the Rosebud, he should thoroughly examine the upper part of Tullock's Creek, and that he should endeavor to send a scout through to Gibbon with the information of the result of this examination. The remainder of the orders is not here in question.

It is not easy to conceive of more explicit orders being given to a detached command, and it will not be pretended by well-informed and trained officers that, in the event of matters being found in the condition anticipated when the orders were given, there can be found one word or hint of authority to depart from them.

Custer's discretion to deviate from them might be exercised:

First. If the condition of things was found to be essentially different from what Terry believed it to be when he issued his orders.

Second. If Custer should see *sufficient reason* for departing from his orders.

All of the evidence known to exist points conclusively to one fact : That in no single particular was the condition of things, as anticipated by Terry, when making the order, in any way different from the condition found by Custer up to the point when the direction taken by the Indian trail was definitely ascertained. At this point, personal examination demonstrated that the conditions actually existed that Terry had so clearly anticipated, namely : It was found (as it appeared to Terry, " almost certain it would be found"), that the trail turned towards the Little Big Horn. Hence there was nothing in this that warranted any deviation from the order. We thus logically arrive at the second case, that there must be " sufficient reason."

Did it exist?

We look in vain in any narrative of the events, we apply in vain to any one having knowledge of the controlling facts, for any reason for departing from the order at this point. Still less is there a scintilla of evidence of any " sufficient reason " for such a deviation from the order as to completely change Terry's plan, and, as the event showed, make the plan impossible.

Exactly what was found to be true, Terry had anticipated would be found to be true! and in that event Custer was left in no doubt what Terry intended he should do, and with no discretion to do otherwise than as ordered—" still proceed southward, perhaps as far as the headwaters of the Tongue," and, at this-critical point, exactly what Terry did not want done, was done, and, instead of "still continuing southward," the trail of the Indians was followed directly to the village, and with such extraordinary haste that there can be no reasonable doubt that Custer had deliberately formed the purpose to follow the trail and attack the village upon reaching it, regardless of where Gibbon's column might be, and without considering that force as a factor in the action!

To an officer of experience, the phraseology that "The Department Commander does not wish to impose upon you precise orders which might hamper your action when nearly in contact with the enemy" can bear no doubtful meaning. Custer was not nearly in contact with the enemy (did not have any knowledge whatever, beyond what was known at the time of his conference with Terry, of the location, or distance to his camp) when, at a point forty miles away from the village, finding the trail turning, as was expected, towards the Little Big Horn, he deliberately followed it instead of going still southward, and so making impossible of accomplishment the hope of Terry, " that the Indians, if upon the Little Horn, may be so nearly inclosed by the two columns that their escape will be impossible." Nor could Custer fail to know that by no possibility could Gibbon be in the position Terry's order contemplated by the time he (Custer) should stir up the Indians to flight or fight, unless, indeed, information of the course of action he had determined to pursue had been dispatched to Gibbon *instanter* (the 24th) and reached Gibbon's camp on Tullock's Creek by midnight.

With such information, and an intimation of urgency, it would have been possible for Gibbon at the head of his veteran 2d and 7th to appear on the field of action by the afternoon of the 25th. Instead of leaving the course of the Tullock and making a most arduous and exhausting march to the Big Horn, Gibbon could then have continued up the Tullock, over a fair route, directly to the Indian village.

Before moving from the mouth of the Rosebud six selected Crow scouts were detached from Gibbon's command, ferried across the Yellowstone, and assigned to Custer, for the special purpose of meeting just such a contingency. They were to act as a medium of communication between the two commands, and it was most specially impressed upon Custer by Terry himself, that, in taking these scouts from Gibbon, who had but twenty-five, while Custer already had forty, they were really for the service of Gibbon's command.

One of the most important of the duties to which Terry directed Custer to apply these scouts was to send word by some of them of the location of the Indian encampment immediately after having certainly determined it. In point of fact three of them were the bearers of that information, but they were not then acting as scouts, but as fugitives, and they started *after* the fight instead of *before* it.

That Custer had determined early in the evening of the 24th to follow the trail leading to the Little Big Horn is clearly shown by a transaction between himself and Captain Varnum, 7th Cavalry, who commanded his scouts. It is best to give this in Captain Varnum's own words:

" We got into camp about dark and I was skirmishing for grub, being pretty well tired out. Custer came to our camp (the scouts') and sat down, holding a confab in the brush with the Crow scouts. Custer then explained to me that the Crows said that on the divide between the Little Horn and the Rosebud there was a high hill with a crow's nest in it where the Crows went when they tried to steal horses from the Sioux. That when it became daylight they could tell by the rising of the smoke whether there were Indians on the Little Big Horn or not. He wanted some intelligent white man to go with these Crows and get from them what they saw and send back word to him. I told him I supposed that meant me, and it ended in my going. I took with me Charles Reynolds, Mich Bouyer, five Crows and eight or ten Rees. Custer said he would move at 11 o'clock at night; I was to go at nine. He would go to the base of the mountains where I was to be, and I was to send him a note as early as possible of what I learned. I got to the Crow's Nest about 2:30 A. M., on the 25th, about 25 miles from where I had left Custer. I threw myself down and fell asleep; but in about three quarters of an hour, or an hour, I was waked up. It was then just daylight. The Indians (Crows) wanted me on the bluff above us. I scrambled up. I saw the two Tepees, spoken of so often, on the branch down which we went to the fight. The Indians tried to show me an immense pony herd in the valley of the Little Big Horn. I couldn't see it. They told me to ' look for worms.' In fact my eyes were pretty sore anyway. I had ridden about seventy miles without sleep and my eyesight was not very good for long range. I sat down and wrote a dispatch to Custer and sent it off at about 4:45. Before the Rees left with the message, however, the smoke of some of Custer's camp-fires was seen about ten miles off, possibly not so far. The Crows were angry at Custer for allowing fires under the circumstances. Custer got my message at about 8 o'clock and started soon after and the dust of his column could be plainly seen as soon as he did so, though not his troops."

It is thus seen that the most ordinary precautions against discovery were not taken and indeed the advertisement of his approach was sufficient to excite the indignation of his scouts. Captain Wallace, 7th Cavalry, in his itinerary of the march states, in speaking of this same camp and time, " General Custer determined to cross the divide that night " (referring to the night of the 24th).

But to come back to our thread. When Custer followed the trail, he knew beyond cavil that the Indians would either flee or fight when he approached them, and unquestionably he knew that in either case Terry had intended that Gibbon should be in position to take part in any event that might arise. Not only did he deliberately disobey Terry's orders, but beyond dispute he knew that in doing so he was neutralizing, or putting Gibbon's command entirely out of the field of action.

That Terry's " plan," as announced at the conference, had the heartily expressed approval of both his principal subordinates is without question. That it was fully comprehended by both is also without question. Under these conditions, no experienced soldier can fail to reach the logical conclusion that, the facts and conclusions upon which it was based being found as expected, and no new and unanticipated conditions arising, there was no choice left to either of them save to follow *strictly* the plan as announced. The duty to " conform " to the expressed " desire " of the commanding general had become absolute.

It is the most specious fallacy to quote Terry's orders as to what Custer might do when nearly in contact with the enemy as justifying antecedent departure from the plan.

Of course, if the plan had been carried out, Custer, at the expected time (the morning of the 26th—not the morning of the 25th) would have found himself " nearly in contact with the enemy," and of course would have had to determine upon such action as the facts then found should demand, but still unquestionably bound to his chief and to the coöperating column by the terms of the previous mutual understanding at the conference. And this liberty to act alone, and to this extent, and no more, would be understood by any loyal subordinate, acting in good faith toward his commander and a coöperating column.

That the purpose of disobedience was entertained by Custer is evinced by another fact, viz.:

He was ordered (and in this no discretion whatever was given him) on his way up the Rosebud, to *thoroughly* examine the upper part of Tullock's Creek, and endeavor to send a scout through to Gibbon's column with the information thus obtained. General Gibbon's quartermaster Lieut. (now Major) Jacobs, employed a scout by the name of Hernandeen for this special purpose. He was sent with Custer's scouts for no other object, but his services were not made use of.

There is a serious ambiguity, which might lead to misconception, in Fry's statement that " Captain Godfrey says that a scout named Hernandeen was selected for this service and he is of the opinion that General Custer would have sent him during the day if the fight had been delayed until early next morning as he at first intended." Selected by whom? Not, as might be inferred, by Custer, but really by General Terry before leaving the Yellowstone. Captain Hare, 7th Cavalry, writes of this as follows " I had Hernandeen with me on the morning of the 25th, and he went into the fight with me. No orders were given me to send him on any detached duty, although he told me that he had expected to carry dispatches."

Godfrey also says : " The scouts, who seemed to be doing their work thoroughly, giving special attention to the right, toward Tullock's Creek, the valley of which was in general view from the divide." This is certainly an error. The distance between the valleys of the Rosebud and Tullock's Fork is too great for such observation. I do not know the source of Captain Godfrey's information, but Lieut. Varnum (now captain), 7th Cavalry, was in command of all the scouts, and necessarily entirely familiar with all the duties required of them and of what they did. He says that in all his instructions from Custer in regard to scouting he never even heard of Tullock's Creek, but was instructed to devote special attention to the opposite side, and that, if any examination whatever was made of the Tullock Valley, it was made without his knowledge and by some one not under his control. No one has been found who made any such examination and the fact that no attempt was made to send scout Hernandeen through to Gibbon's column is conclusive that this part of the order was absolutely ignored.

Fry admits that Custer did not examine the upper part of Tullock's Creek, but tosses the whole matter aside as colorless, because there were no Indians there and that nothing concerning Tullock's Creek is material in the campaign. As a part of the disobedience, as an important part in that no scout was sent to Gibbon, and as a clear index to the ultimate purpose, it is very far from colorless or unimportant.

Why should that order have been ignored if Custer had intended that Gibbon, and Terry, who was with Gibbon's command, should have information of his movements? Clearly he did not so intend, and certainly this was in entire accord with the purpose he had in contemplation when in St. Paul, and which, on this, the first opportunity which had occurred, he so fatally carried out—to "cut loose from Terry at the first chance."

But even this grave disobedience is swallowed up in the magnitude of that which General Fry has attempted to defend, and which involved not only the fate of a campaign, but the fate of almost a regiment of as gallant and loyal men as ever went into battle.

A well-matured plan, based on reasonable conclusions from known facts, contemplating the coöperative action of two bodies of troops, intending to bring them into joint action at a specific date and place,—the purpose explained not alone in the written orders, but in full conference of all the commanders—is defeated by the failure of one column to carry out its assigned share, and this failure not caused by unforeseen conditions found to exist by its commander, while in its execution, but because he followed the trail directly, which he was certainly " desirea," if not actually forbidden NOT *to do, and arrrived at the point of coöperation thirty-six hours in advance of the appointed time.*

In this there was willful disobedience, and there was hardly less culpable neglect of duty in the fact that no attempt was made to send to Terry, whose position was known and easily reached, one word of information that the whole plan of the march of that column was changed and that it would be on the appointed ground on the morning of the 25th instead of the afternoon of the 26th.

Before quitting this feature of the case, let us see how General Gibbon put himself on record on this subject. In transmitting the map of his itineraryist, from Fort Shaw, M. T., November 6th, 1876, he writes as follows :

"So great was my fear that Custer's zeal would carry him forward too rapidly that the last thing I said to him when bidding him good bye after his regiment had filed past you when starting on his march was, 'Now, Custer, don't be greedy, but wait for us.' He replied gaily, as with a wave of his hand he dashed off to follow his regiment, 'No, I will not.' Poor fellow ! Knowing what we do now, and what an effect a fresh Indian trail seemed to have had upon him, *perhaps we were expecting too much to anticipate a forbearance on his part which would have rendered cöoperation of the two columns practicable.*

" Except so far as to draw profit trom past experience it is perhaps useless to speculate as to what would have been the result had your plan, as originally agreed upon, been carried out. But I cannot help reflecting that in that case my column, supposing the Indian camp to have remained where it was when Custer struck it, would have been the first to reach it, that with our infantry and Gatling guns we should have been able to take care of ourselves, even though numbering only about two-thirds of Custer's force, and that with six hundred cavalry in the neighborhood, led as only Custer could lead it, the result to the Indians would have been very different from what it was. * * * "

But to continue, Fry says : " The utter failure of our campaign was due to underestimating the number and prowess of the enemy," and, in this, he quotes Gibbon (but only in part) and wholly fails to distinguish between a " check " and such a disaster as the massacre of five troops of cavalry.

Crook had had a " check," but no massacre, and even the remainder of Custer's column was able to hold out against the victory flushed Indians until Terry and Gibbon came up. Then, notwithstanding the fact that this latter force numbered but four hundred men, and the Indian force was practically untouched, they incontinently fled. Is it not easily conceivable that, had Gibbon and Custer been acting together, as Terry had planned, the force would certainly have had no " check," much less an overwhelming disaster, if indeed it failed of a signal victory? Even if Custer's whole body of troops had been together it is most probable that no such disaster could have occurred. Indeed it is well established that, at the inception of Custer's attack, the Indians began packing up and preparing to fly, some of them actually leaving the field, and, doubtless, the signs of this purpose, which Custer could easily observe from the high hills he was on, led him to believe that the village was in full flight, and prompted his hasty and disastrous attack on the village from the north.

It may not be out of place here to quote what the late Lieutenant General P. H. Sheridan has said officially on this subject :

" Had the Seventh Cavalry been kept together it is mv belief it would have been able to handle the Indians on the Little Big Horn, and under any circumstances it could have at least defended itself ; but separated as it was into three detachments, the Indians had largely the advantage, in addition to their overwhelming numbers "

---

* Tne italics are my own. R. H. P.

But for the fact that General Fry's comments, of which the avowed purpose was to show that Custer had not disobeyed, have had injected into them a severe criticism of Terry's military operations and plan, the purpose of this paper would be accomplished. This, however, makes it necessary to discuss the criticism.

Fry thinly veils the spirit underlying his criticisms by crediting Terry with being "one of the best of men and ablest of soldiers." Less than that he could hardly have said of a man of such high ability as a soldier and of such preëminent virtues as a man.

The criticism upon the facts, as Fry states them, falls to the ground in view of the fact that it is not based on what really was the plan and the operations.

Throughout the comments, he assumes that the " plan " (which it is also assumed Terry gave but little thought to at the time) was conceived and concluded at the conference, and that it was the joint work of Terry, Gibbon and Custer. It is spoken of as the " conference plan "—" the plan decided upon in conference "— and to sustain this assumption it is asserted that Terry says in his annual report of 1876 that he " decided upon a plan at the conference of June 21st." He also locates Gibbon's force "some fifteen miles up the Yellowstone nearly opposite the mouth of the Big Horn "; the Rosebud and Big Horn are put " about fifteen miles apart "; and it is left to be inferred that the only facts upon which a plan could be formed was that " a scouting party had found indications that the Indians were on the Big Horn or its tributaries."

It is further asserted that Terry had " about 1000 men on the south bank of the Yellowstone at the mouth of the Rosebud on June 21st "; that " on the night of June 21st Terry held a conference with Gibbon and Custer."

No one of these statements is correct.

From the very beginning Terry planned to employ the cavalry as his strategic and fighting force, holding an infantry support within reach. Until he came into communication with Gibbon's column he had maintained this support with the train and at the supply depot. When he reached the mouth of the Tongue and had brought the two commands into communication he so modified his original plans as to provide in future operations that the two columns should afford mutual support, and depend upon pack-mule transportation.

Terry learned through an Indian of the result of Reno's scout and approximately, of his whereabouts, at the mouth of the Tongue, late in the evening of June 19th. That night I rode through to Reno's bivouac, which was in the direction of our proposed operations, with orders for him to remain there and rest his men and animals the next day while Custer should bring up the remainder of the 7th, the scouts and Low's battery. On the night of the 20th Custer bivouacked with Reno. After my return to Terry on the night of the 19th, with such information as I had gathered, the maps were gotten out and the general field gone over. A copy of the map then extant of that region accompanies this paper. It will be observed that the Rosebud was an unexplored and unmapped region. (See pages 24 and 25.)

Terry reached Reno's bivouac during the morning of the 20th. After collecting all available information, the measures to be taken were discussed and the " plan " in its general features determined upon, and Custer was told that afternoon of the work laid out for him, and cautioned to husband the forces of his men and animals. The same evening, leaving Custer to bring up this command, Terry proceeded up the Yellowstone on the steamer *Far West*, reaching Gibbon's camp, which was four miles below the mouth of the Rosebud. Before noon of the 21st, Gibbon's column was put in motion up the north bank of the Yellowstone pursuant to Terry's plan, within an hour after he had arrived, and before Custer's command had reached the mouth of the Rosebud on the south side. Thus it will be seen that Gibbon's troops were measuring the road to the mouth of the Big Horn—which they found to be sixty miles instead of fifteen as stated in the " comments "—pursuant to the "plan," before Custer, who was marching, with his command, could possibly take part in the conference.

Custer and command arrived at the Rosebud at about 2 P. M. Soon thereafter the conference was held. After its close, Low's battery was ferried across to the north bank to overtake and join Gibbon's column, and half a dozen Crows were carried to the south side. Thus we see that the command on the south bank of the Yellowstone is reduced to the command that Custer took to the Little Big Horn, which, omitting the scouts, Fry estimates elsewhere at six hundred, which is very nearly correct.

It would naturally be inferred from the statement in the " comments " that Terry's belief that the Indians were on the Little Big Horn was based solely upon the report of a scouting

party which had found "indications," and thus leaves the inference that Terry had no facts from which to reach sound conclusions, and upon which to form a well considered plan. The only
scouting party, south of the Yellowstone, had been Reno's, and
he reported "heavy Indian trails leading up the Rosebud." But
besides this Terry had full information as to the object of this
great gathering of Indians, and knowledge of the usual place of
assemblage. He also had, before drawing up his letter of instructions, reports from Gibbon's Crow scouts to the effect that
they had seen "many smokes" on the Little Big Horn. He had
the benefit of the zealous services of such skilled scouts as Mitch
Bouyer and Charles Reynolds,—men who thoroughly knew the
country and the Indians (the former being one himself), their
habits and their accustomed haunts. From all of these facts,
Terry had reached the definite conclusions, so well verified later,
that the Indians were in large numbers, were together or in contiguous camps, and were either on the Little Big Horn or the
Rotten Grass.

It was on these conclusions that Terry's "plan" (his own and
not a conference plan) was based and definitely made *before* and
not *at* the conference. It was only determined upon after carefully weighing the possibilities of other projects and a free discussion of the situation with members of his staff.

Terry's report of 1876 does not furnish any warrant for the
statement that the plan was made at the conference, but, on the
contrary, and which is *most decidedly different*, he says, "at the
conference I communicated to them the plan of operations which
I had decided to adopt."

It is certain, on Terry's authority, that at the conference, he
offered, if Custer so wished, to modify his plan and give him
(Custer) all of the cavalry (four troops of the old 2d were with
Gibbon), but he objected and it was not done. It is possible that
some matters of minor detail may have been changed and modified at the conference—and certainly a few changes in the per-
sonnel were made—but one thing is perfectly clear: the "plan"
came to the conference fully matured in Terry's mind (and it had
been outlined to Custer before leaving his camp of the night before) and had to Terry *at that time* all the "force" and "importance" that it ever acquired.

These errors of statement as to position of troops, distances
between important points, information as to Indians, and, above

all, misquotations of Terry's official report are all necessary to give a color of probability to the *assumption* that it was a " conference plan," and that to Terry its " force " and " importance " were an afterthought,—which, if it were true, would be as discreditable to his ability as a soldier as to his integrity as a man.

This plan was fully explained by Terry to both Custer and Gibbon on the afternoon of June 21st. That it was perfectly understood by them even Fry does not question. That success would have resulted from following it can only be conjectured as probable, but it can be certainly said that Custer's disaster could not have happened in that event.

It has been shown that the plan was maturely considered, clearly formulated and well understood. Gibbon so states, and Terry's report, which Fry misquotes, leaves it beyond cavil.

This plan, in its detail, was formed immediately after his becoming acquainted with the information which Reno brought back, of the existence and direction of the Indian trail.

That the general features of any specific operations, which might take place if the Indians were found, were already formulated in Terry's mind long before is abundantly indicated in many ways, not alone by his conversations, but such passages as the following from his letter to Gibbon dated as early as February 26th. In this, after many details as to other matters, he says:

" In fact prepare the project of a campaign down the Yellowstone Valley on the theory that Crook is coming up from the south, and that you and Custer must prevent the Sioux from getting away to the northward, and then turn in and help Crook give them a whipping."

In the conversation at the mouth of the Rosebud, when the plan was announced and discussed, Terry said: " It must be assumed that Crook is somewhere in reach along the base of the Big Horn mountains," and later along in the same conversation, " I will not leave the infantry out of the fight."

Now it is plain that the general features of the plan were clear in Terry's mind from the first. He expected to find the Indians about where they were finally found. He expected to find them (as they were finally found) " concentrated in contiguous camps." He expected to find them in such large force that five hundred and fifty cavalry would " run great risk of defeat " in attacking them. He expected to find Crook with his force in position to prevent the escape of the Indians from his own command. In all of these particulars, his anticipations were realized.

How utterly absurd then when he got such further knowledge of the Indians as convinced him that all of his conjectures were right to allege that his "plan" had so little thought, purpose and cohe sion that it only assumed importance in his mind *after* the disaster

The definite plan which was given to Gibbon and Custer was based on Reno's discoveries and on the stated opinions and known facts of such experienced Indian scouts as Bouyer, Reynolds, Gerard and others, who were with him. It contemplated a *joint*, or combined operation of the two columns—not independent movement—and what the final event showed to be of more consequence than all other features, it contemplated taking no chances of defeat by attacking known superiority of force with insufficient means.

It should be noted here that Custer's total force when he left Terry was only about one hundred greater than the five hundred and fifty which Terry had said in February were too few with which to attack " without great ri.k of defeat."

It is difficult to consider with patience the groundless assumption that Terry had in reality no well-defined plan, and that what he clearly ordered and verbally discussed with Gibbon and Custer only found importance in his mind when disaster had come.

The gist of the plan, as already stated, was to direct the movements of the two columns in such a way that if the Indians fled they could not escape to the southeast without being driven upon Crook; they could not go westward because they were already near the eastern bank of the Big Horn River and the eastern boundary of the territory of the Crow Nation with whom they were in open hostility; northward they would be met by Gibbon, and the Big Horn mountains lie to the southward, in which they could not have maintained themselves for any considerable time if they once permitted themselves to be cooped up in them.

If they made a stand, the purpose is clearly set forth in Terry's report: Custer was to keep on southward (after determining where the trail led), for the double purpose of intercepting flight if it should be attempted, but above all to so manœuvre his strategic column as to give time for Gibbon's column to come up. This plan was founded on the belief that the two columns might be brought into coöperating distance of each other. Or as Gibbon states it in his letter of November 6th, previously referred to.

"I saw Custer depart on the 22d with his fine regiment fully impressed with the conviction that our chief aim should be to so move that whatever force might be on the Little Big Horn should not escape us. * * * And it was fully understood between us that *to give my troops time to get up,* and to *guard against escape of the Indians to the South,** he should keep constantly feeling to his left."

It should be borne in mind that these operations were directed against a village community; that the fighting force of this community could not leave their village to go out to attack one of the approaching columns without abandoning their wives, children and property an easy prey to the other.

It must be remembered further that half of Gibbon's force consisted of infantry; that the conditions required that he should take the longest route to the objective, thus making it impossible for him to reach coöperating distance unless Custer manœuvred for delay. It was well understood that Gibbon could not be in place without resorting to forced marches, before the 26th at the earliest, and also well understood that if Custer marched as directed he would, at the same time, be, where it was intended he should be, "in coöperating distance," on the only possible line of retreat if the Indians should run away, while if they held their ground and fought he would be able to make his attack a joint one with Gibbon.

Custer made a forced march and held to the Indian trail instead of moving still southward, and this brought him on the night of the 24th into the position he ought to have occupied on the morning of the 26th, and at least twenty-four hours before Gibbon could possibly be expected to be in place. The fact that Custer did not have any new information concerning the hostile Indians when he began forcing the pace is put beyond question by Capt. Varnum in the letter heretofore quoted.

It is mere sophistry to quote Sherman as saying that "when Custer found himself in the presence of the Indians, he could do nothing but attack" as justification for Custer. That is conceded, but it still remains that Custer had no business to be *at that time* "in the presence of the Indians," and had he not flagrantly disobeyed the plain language and still more flagrantly the perfectly understood purpose and "spirit" of his orders, he *would not have been there.*

It is in no way necessary to discuss the battle tactics adopted

---

* The italics are mine.—R. P. H.

by Custer when he attacked the village. We leave that to others. What he did when he attacked the villages may have been very judicious, in view of what he then knew and saw. It certainly lacked nothing of his usual boldness. Everything indicates that he was convinced that the Indians were in full flight, and, if this were true, his tactics are not to be criticised.

Mistakes or bad tactics, on his part, at that time, are not under discussion and are of no moment here—the trouble lay in the fact that he found himself where his orders forbade him to be at that time!

As Terry had anticipated in February, the Indians were in one camp, and the force attacking was so small that it not only ran the risk of defeat, but was most disastrously defeated.

There is neither occasion nor disposition here to find fault with what Custer did when he found himself compelled to act *alone* when it had been intended that Gibbon should be practically *with him*. The only criticism I make is that he was not in the place his orders directed him to be.

There must be no confusion between the disobedience which made the disaster possible, and the fact of the disaster itself.

The only reason for speaking here of Custer's battle tactics is found in the fact that even in that Fry attempts to criticise Terry.

Fry's explanation of Custer's battle tactics in detaching Benteen with three troops to the south, as being done "no doubt in deference to Terry's advice," is wholly gratuitous. In all that Terry ordered or advised, there is no thought, expressed or implied, which could be supposed to control Custer's battle tactics. What Custer was to do at the head of the Rosebud, more than a day before the fight, and more than forty miles away from where it finally took place, in case he should find the trail going towards the Little Big Horn, namely, continue southward, can by no possibility be made to apply to his action when he was in face of the enemy.

Whatever was in Custer's mind when he found he must attack —whether he did or did not misjudge what he saw; whether with his information he acted wisely or unwisely in detaching Benteen can never be known. But certainly nothing could be more absurd than to believe that he was influenced in doing so by his instructions from Terry.

It is idle to take such great pains to show that Custer's march was not unduly rapid. This is simply mystifying and leading away from the real issue, which is not whether Custer reached the Indian village with men and horses exhausted, but whether the march was not in direct defiance of his orders. Fry says: "The trouble was their strength was underestimated. Terry reported July 2d: 'He (Custer) expressed the utmost confidence he had all the force he could need, and I shared his confidence.'" How unfair and misleading Fry's quotation is is plain in view of the fact that no such condition of things as Custer brought about by his disobedience was contemplated by Terry when he left him. It was not supposed for a moment that he would march directly upon and attack the village so long before it was possible for Gibbon to be in place. It was known that he understood the plan, and that he understood his orders, and it was supposed that he would obey them. For this "understood" purpose Terry believed and agreed with him, that his force was ample. Hence it is of no importance whether the Indians were underestimated or not, for no matter what estimate was made of the Indian numbers, Custer's force was abundant to have enabled him to obey his orders.

It was not ample, as Terry had foreseen, to meet a contingency not contemplated, and which could not have arisen had his orders been adhered to.

We need go no further than the story of what occurred after the annihilation of Custer to make it perfectly clear that his force was ample for all that he was instructed to do. This may be very briefly stated. Reno's attack was a miserable failure, ending in a disorderly rout and a scramble for the hills, where the cool head and noted courage of Benteen saved the two battalions from a disaster even greater than had occurred to Custer. After sweeping Custer's five troops from the field, and encouraged by the victory obtained over Reno's battalion, the Indians swarmed down upon the now assembled force in overwhelming numbers, evidently very confident that it was only a question of a few hours when it too would be forced to submit to the same fate that had befallen the other. But in this they were mistaken. Benteen was a factor they had overlooked, and, notwithstanding the disadvantages of the position, the embarrassments incident to the care of the wounded, total lack of water in the camp, which could be obtained from the river only at possible loss of life, this remnant held out until Gibbon's command came in sight, when the whole body of the Indians abandoned the field.

It may be well to note that Gibbon's command was sighted by the Indians at the very time the "plan" contemplated it would be. Let it be assumed that Custer's command had been maintained intact, fresh and eager for work, led as he could have, and certainly did lead it—with a dauntless courage and a vigorous boldness of attack—and Gibbon with his column of old, war-tried, well-seasoned veterans equally well led,—if both had simultaneously reached their point of combined work and simultaneously advanced against the Indians, is it too much to believe that one of the most brilliant victories over the Indians would have been won?

Plainly the whole event and all its parts show that no wiser or more successful plan could have been devised for bringing the Indians to a contest of strength; no anticipation of unknown events could have been keener or more accurate; no more fruitful possibilities could have been realized. Even in case the very worst had happened and the Indians had fled, they would have been closely followed by Terry's whole force and must have been driven directly into Crook's force, or cooped up in the Big Horn mountains.

In the final paragraph of the "Comments," it is stated: "On the 30th of July a staff officer arrived at Terry's camp with orders for Terry and Crook to unite. After their junction—August 10th—there was much marching but no fighting." The staff officer referred to was General James W. Forsyth, and the "orders" he brought were as follows:

"Brigadier Genl. A. H. Terry,   "Chicago, July 20th, 1876.
    "Care of Lieut. Col. Jas. W. Forsyth.

"I send General Forsyth to consult with you. I have made arrangements for the construction of the two posts on the Yellowstone. They are to be similar to Fort Lincoln and everything will be sent to the ground so that all now necessary is to know the points and to have the hostile Indians hit so that we can get a sufficient number of troops to guard the workmen. I therefore advise you to make arrangements to form a junction with General Crook unless you feel strong enough yourself to defeat the hostile Indians, when all your troops are up. We cannot send any more troops nor would it be reasonable to send more if it is at all practicable for Crook and yourself to unite. Colonel Merritt reports that very few if any Indians have left the agencies since Custer's fight. The military posts are to be for six companies of cavalry and five companies of infantry each. In other words will be for the accommodation of two regiments, one of cavalry one of infantry.   (Signed)   P. H. Sheridan,
                                    "Lieutenant General."

It is to be noted that, in this letter, the words "I therefore advise" are granted to convey an "order," while it is contended that Terry's "he desires that you should conform" are not an order. The inconsistency need not be remarked upon. With other matters in which the comments and even Godfrey's article itself might well be the subject of remark, I do not concern myself. My sole purpose here has been to show:

First: That Dr. Munger's remark, to which so much exception was taken, is just and true, and was fully warranted by the facts; and

Second: That the criticism of Terry by Fry, when it is not misapprehension of facts, is an attribution of fault where none existed.

I have very deeply regretted the necessity of saying anything concerning this matter, but being compelled to speak I was not willing to issue anything without making a careful review of the papers in order that I might be fully sustained in what I said by the records, and by the testimony of those who knew, and thus put the facts beyond question. The endeavor has been to let the documents tell the story, and to limit the other work as nearly as might be to indicating simply the proper connection or to such remarks as would insure a perfect understanding.

For reasons before given, this has imposed a long and difficult task upon me, which no feeling of resentment arising from the fact that I was personally assailed would have prompted, and no personal defense would have repaid.

I have been thoroughly conversant all these years with the noble and generous sacrifice, the complete abnegation of self that General Terry knowingly made for the avowed purpose of shielding a dead man from public blame. I have seen him receive thrust after thrust, year after year, on this matter, and quietly ignore it with some such remark as "Blinder Eifer schadet nur." But when this striking example of his main characteristic was cited in his praise at his bier, and I find the facts denied, the sacrifice and consequent suffering scoffed at, and the magnanimous man himself arrogantly and ignorantly criticised and adroitly belittled, both as man and soldier, it becomes a duty to expose facts enough to meet the case.

I have endeavored to limit the field of discussion to simply meeting all aggressive points of attack, and it is only because it seemed necessary, in defense of the memory of an able soldier, the kindest and noblest-hearted man I have ever known, that I have permitted myself to say what I have.

In no way do I intend or desire to assail General Custer, but it has been forced upon me that his error in disobeying the orders of his superior must be made plain. What reasons he had,—what justification he might have shown, are known to no one living.

As General Terry said in his confidential report of July 2d;

"I do not tell you this to cast any reflection on Custer. For whatever errors he may have committed he has paid the penalty, and you cannot regret his loss more than I do, but I felt that our plan must have been successful had it been carried out, and I desire you to know the facts."